Corporate Restructuring

Corporate Restructuring
Managing the Change Process from Within

Gordon Donaldson
Harvard Business School

Harvard Business School Press
Boston, Massachusetts

The paper used in this publication meets the requirements of the American
National Standard for Permanence of Paper for Printed Library Materials Z39.49-1984.

LIBRARY OF CONGRESS CATALOGING-IN-PUBLICATION DATA
Donaldson, Gordon, 1922–
    Corporate restructuring : managing the change process from within /
Gordon Donaldson.
        p.   cm.
    Includes bibliographical references and index.
    ISBN 0-87584-339-5
    1. Corporations—United States—Finance—Case studies.
    2. Corporate reorganizations—United States—Management—Case studies.   I. Title.
HG4061.D578   1994
658.1'6—dc20   93-30462
                                                              CIP

To my wife, Joan,
our children,
and grandchildren

Contents

Acknowledgments

I want to express my sincere appreciation to the many individuals whose cooperation and support were essential to the completion of this study. First and foremost, I wish to thank the senior executives of the cooperating companies who made their experience accessible to me without reservation. Without their trust that the findings would be reported accurately and objectively, the research could not have been undertaken.

In the assembly and analysis of the company data I was ably assisted by Scott Sucher and Chris Allen whose careful and resourceful work laid a foundation for my understanding of the information provided. I would also like to thank Connie Rodrigues and Dale Abramson who worked on endless revisions of the manuscript with unfailing care and good humor.

The advice of editors and reviewers is always an important but unseen influence on books attributed to a single author. I wish to acknowledge, in particular, that the manuscript benefited greatly from the advice of my principal editor, Carol Franco, and from a provocative review by William Taylor. The case history of General Mills in Chapter 6 received an initial editing by Richard Ruback for the *Journal of Financial Economics* and by Donald Chew for the *Journal of Applied Corporate Finance*, which then served to help shape the other two detailed case histories in Chapters 7 and 8.

I would also like to acknowledge the financial and moral support received from the Division of Research of the Harvard Business School, and, in particular, from its director, F. Warren McFarlan, over the more than six years this study has been in the making. It is greatly appreciated.

Finally, I would like to acknowledge the influence of the vast volume of published work on this subject which has preceded this publication, from which I have benefited. I can only be partially aware of the impact it has had on the ideas expressed herein.

PART I

The Nature and Origin
of Structural Change

CHAPTER 1

Introduction

A Decade of Confrontation

The primary purpose of this book is to set the financial restructuring that dominated the corporate scene in the last decade in the perspective of the evolution of financial strategy and structure since World War II and to assess its impact on the management of large-scale industrial firms. Many believe that there has been a fundamental and lasting change in corporate priorities as professional investors have reasserted the traditional rights of ownership over the prerogatives conferred on or assumed by professional management. The question is: How fundamental, and how lasting?

The 1980s will be remembered in the annals of corporate America as the decade of confrontation. Managers whose claim to leadership was based on a lifetime of corporate service were under attack from external critics who asserted a widening gap between investor expectations and corporate performance. Charges of incompetence, inefficiency, indifference, wastefulness, and self-dealing were used to arouse a traditionally passive shareholder electorate to vote for new leadership. In the political vernacular of the 1990s—it was time for a change.

To those who had grown up in an era when the professionalization of business management in America had been hailed as a home-grown national treasure and a unique competitive advantage for the second half of the twentieth century, this came as a shock. The drama of a rising tide of corporate takeovers caught the public attention: corporate gladiators fighting to the death before an audience eager for the promised riches of escalating equity values. The business press seized on the excitement of the struggle for personal power and potential wealth to bring corporate affairs into the range of vision of the average citizen far beyond what had ever occurred. Hitherto unfamiliar corporate names and anonymous corporate leaders, obscure individuals suddenly appearing as sinister "raiders," Wall Street money managers, all became part of the weekly news parade of personalities involved in companies under siege.

Two of many well-known examples can be used to mark the beginning and the end of this decade of corporate restructuring. One of the most notorious takeover attempts occurred in 1982, when William Agee, chief executive officer of Bendix, launched his bid to acquire Martin Marietta. Both companies were conglomerates, one with its origins in automotive parts and the other in aircraft. The objective was to merge and reassemble the components of these two companies into a new superconglomerate, thereby to create new value for Bendix shareholders.

At stake was the independence and control of Martin Marietta. J. Donald Rauth, its CEO, and Thomas Pownall, its president and later CEO, did what all incumbents do under the circumstances— they fought back. Tipped off by Wall Street insiders that a takeover was being planned, the Martin Marietta board and management were prepared for rapid response. In the summer of 1981, Martin Marietta had placed Kidder Peabody on retainer for this purpose and had done preliminary valuation work. The ensuing battle founded a new lexicon of corporate warfare in which the colorful twentieth-century imagery of Pac-Man defenses, poison pills, and golden parachutes merged with that of medieval knights in armor—white and black—in the role of rescuer or villain.

Martin Marietta reacted with a counterbid to take over Bendix, in the process of which both companies took on enormous burdens of debt servicing in order to acquire large fractions of each other's stock. Third and fourth parties were drawn into the struggle for ultimate control, and in the end it was the intervention of Edward Hennessy of Allied Corporation which, in taking over control of an outmaneuvered Bendix, forced Bendix to relax its grip on Martin Marietta and allow it to go free. After the settlement, Allied owned

slightly less than 40% of Martin Marietta, subject to optional repurchase by Martin Marietta, which was subsequently accomplished.

This episode could be written off as one of many examples of a
highly personal power struggle having little to do with the fundamental purposes of corporate activity. At a more fundamental level, however, it illustrated a growing perception that many business organizations in the 1980s had become vulnerable to a challenge to leadership
because their strategy and structure were increasingly inconsistent
with the product and capital-market environment of the time.

In Martin Marietta's case, the company that had been formed in
1961 by a merger of the Martin Company (aircraft, aerospace, and
missiles) and American Marietta (building materials) was a classic
conglomerate. The inherent clash of corporate markets and cultures
was never effectively resolved, and an unresolved internal debate as
to how to rationalize the disparate corporate entities and refocus the
company persisted. As one Martin Marietta executive put it, Bendix's
hostile takeover attempt had the unintended effect of collapsing the
internal debate and uniting management in the defense of its collective
turf: "It took away all the argument." In the process of defense, the
accumulation of a heavy debt burden produced a discipline of its
own, which forced the rapid liquidation of peripheral businesses and
a refocus on aerospace as Martin Marietta's primary competitive franchise. Some Martin Marietta managers privately agreed that, though
unintended and unappreciated at the time, Agee's attack had a positive and beneficial outcome.

The era of confrontation from without the corporate organization, which the nation observed through the public press, was also
marked by an off-camera confrontation from within. The tensions
created by business strategies and structures out of sync with the
product and capital-market environment produced intracorporate initiatives to change direction, which at times had equally dramatic results. One of these occurred at the end of the decade within the board
of directors of General Motors. The intractable problems facing the
leading U.S. automaker, evident in eroding competitive position and
financial performance, were forcefully brought to public attention by
the acquisition of Electronic Data Systems as a subsidiary and H.
Ross Perot as a board member. His disagreement with Roger Smith
over the direction of the company ended with Perot's resignation from
the board and the purchase of his stock by General Motors.

Then, in April of 1992, a ten-year veteran of General Motors'
board, John Smale, former CEO of Procter & Gamble, asserted the

leadership of the outside board members to nominate himself as chairman of the board's executive committee, replacing Robert Stempel, GM's board chairman and CEO. The concurrent appointment of John Smith as GM's new president and chief operating officer was evidence of a new board activism and Smale's leadership in attempting to restructure and reinvigorate the ailing giant. Within six months Stempel resigned and was succeeded by Smith as CEO and Smale as chairman of the board.

Though these examples of restructuring initiatives and others like them may now be the public stereotype of modern corporate governance, few would argue that either of them illustrates how the system ought to work. Clearly, in each case, the normal structure of governance under which shareholders delegate to a board of directors and a board delegates to executive officers the responsibility to shape and reshape a successful strategy and structure had failed to prevent a performance shortfall large and persistent enough to attract radical and risky intervention. While it can be argued that the General Motors episode reflected a board doing the job it was appointed to do, it is nonetheless an example of a crisis-induced act of last resort. Surely if either external or internal confrontation has become the common means by which large, mature corporations adapt to change, the established governance system has failed.

Are these cases typical? In an attempt to answer that question, and to provide a more balanced perspective, this book examines the working of the corporate governance system across a varied sample of voluntary and involuntary restructurings in the 1980s. It describes examples of both success and failure of corporate self-governance and attempts to learn from this experience how to improve on the modern governance process.

Financial Structure as an Instrument of Change

We have become so familiar with the phrase "financial restructuring" in the past decade that we often fail to ask why financial structure became such a battleground for contending agents of change and such a compelling target of reform. The answer lies in the function of structure and in the way it influences the actual and potential payoffs from private, profit-making enterprise.

The word "structure," used in an economic context, implies a specific, stable relationship among the key elements of a particular function or process. Financial structure refers to the allocation of the corporate flow of funds—cash or credit—and to the strategic or contractual decision rules that direct the flow and determine the value-added and its distribution among the various corporate constituencies. The elements of the corporate financial structure include the scale of the investment base, the mix between active investment and defensive reserves, the focus of investment (choice of revenue source), the rate at which earnings are reinvested, the mix of debt and equity contracts, the nature, degree, and cost of corporate oversight (overhead), the distribution of expenditures between current and future revenue potential, and the nature and duration of wage and benefit contracts.

To refer to these as elements of financial structure implies a limited and inflexible range of options and hints at the problem that restructuring is designed to address. We know that the economic phenomena which bear on the pattern of corporate funds flows are dynamic and constantly evolving. On the other hand, it is a fact of management and organizational behavior that most, if not all, of these elements which affect the pattern of funds flows are subject to constraints over extended periods of time imposed by a particular business mission and strategy. Stability or continuity in financial structure is essential to the implementation of a stable and predictable set of payoffs among the various corporate constituencies, including shareholders, united behind the chosen strategic plan.

However, even if the strategic plan proves to have been optimal at the time, it is subject to a changing environment. Changes in consumer demand, in competitors' response in the national and world economies, in the capital markets, in constituency power and priorities, in government regulation and stimulus, all guarantee that a given financial structure will not remain right forever. And since it is designed in the expectation of stability and continuity, it often tends to outstay its welcome. Hence the 1980s.

Financial structure is by nature strategically passive. It does not define a corporate strategy; it is merely an instrument of that strategy. It is a kind of control panel for a corporate space vehicle whose switches, buttons, and levers are adjusted when a new direction is set. Thus, one of the first objectives of a new mission leader is to gain control of that panel to quickly and fundamentally alter the course of corporate funds flows to accord with the new strategic plan. It is not surprising that a new strategic direction shows itself first as financial restructuring even though the latter is merely a means to the end.

Some Questions about Restructuring in the 1980s

In view of the fact that the concept of a stable financial structure is inconsistent with an evolving environment, it is not surprising that individual corporations experience a periodic restructuring process. Observations of corporate history suggest that this happens on the order of once a decade or so. But why, as in the 1980s, the timing of restructuring coincided for so many companies and took on epidemic proportions is not so obvious. The experience of the 1980s raises a host of questions about the phenomenon, which has prompted this study. The following questions have guided its agenda.

The first question arises from the harsh criticism that has been heaped on U.S. corporate leadership by champions of the stockholder interest who saw the decade of the 1970s as an era of mismanagement in pursuit of misguided or self-serving corporate objectives. If the alleged destruction of shareholder value was so great and so obvious, how was it that chief executives and boards of directors elected to represent the shareholder interest could get so far out of touch with their electorate for so long? More specifically, if the corporate strategy and structure in place in 1980 was so patently wrong for the 1980s, why was it perceived to be right for the 1970s or 1960s?

One answer, offered by some critics among the press, academics, and corporate activists, is that the offending strategy and structure were never right, that they existed because professional managers, whether through ignorance, neglect, or self-serving ambition, are not naturally disposed to pursue financial efficiency aggressively. Without denying the evidence that ignorance, neglect, and self-interest play a part in the behavior of managers, as in other areas of human endeavor, there is an alternative hypothesis. It is that corporate strategy and structure are shaped by the internal and external environment of the time and may therefore have been quite appropriate at their inception. However, as I have suggested, any stable structure in time outlives its relevance for the current environment.

This book explores the origins of the 1960s and 1970s financial structure, which was so aggressively restructured in the 1980s: how and why it came into being, why it was perceived as being right for the time, and why it ceased to represent a proper framework for future corporate decisions and action. The conclusion reached is that the post–World War II strategies of the companies under observation were by and large an intelligent and rational response to the stimuli transmitted to management from the internal and external environment at the time. Only later did the inherent inertia of large organizations lead to a failure to respond in a timely manner to a changed environment and to a strategy and structure open to serious challenge.

One of the findings of this study, which will become evident to the reader, is that the problems which the 1980s restructuring was designed to address did not emerge suddenly, but developed gradually and cumulatively over the span of a decade or more. Thus the elements of corporate performance labeled in the 1980s by critics as gross abuses of executive power were becoming apparent during the 1970s. This being the case, where was the voice of the injured parties and their capital-market intermediaries in the 1970s and where were the financial press and the analysts who should have been calling for remedial action?

Considering the coverage of individual companies by security analysts and the press through this period for signs of growing dissent, one realizes that capital-market signals, like those emitted by the physical universe, come from many sources, vary in strength and persistence, and reflect different stimuli. Except in extreme cases, they are open to different interpretations, some of which challenge and others reinforce the existing theory of the corporate universe in the minds of management. Receiving these signals in real time of the 1960s and 1970s, even the objective observer found it difficult to detect a clear and unequivocal mandate for change. Only in retrospect is this cumulative evidence unassailable. In this uncertain environment it is not surprising, therefore, that corporate leaders heard what they wanted to hear, and filtered out the dissonance.

If environmental change is a gradual process, which normally emerges over a five- or ten-year time span, why is the response to change in corporate strategy and structure not also a gradual and continuous process; why is it so often episodic and convulsive? Examining the case histories of a number of companies over a span of 20 or more years enables one to observe the specific causes and consequences of particular financial structures and the circumstances leading to a process of change.

Two conclusions become obvious in reviewing these experiences. One is that no organization can tolerate more than one vision of the future at a time. Each chief executive brings his or her unique vision to leadership, and in the large and mature enterprise it takes an extended period of time to communicate that vision, to gain collective commitment, and to develop detailed and effective implementation. The other is that once in place, the strategy and structure which reflect that vision take on a life of their own and develop a loyal constituency with a vested interest in perpetuating the payoff.

Hence resistance to change often preserves the status quo well beyond its period of relevance so that when change comes, the pent-up forces, like an earthquake, capture in one violent moment a decade of gradual change. The question becomes not, Why is adaptation to change not more continuous? but, Why does voluntary change happen at all, except in convulsive shocks? What circumstances and processes allow a mature corporation to change course under a normal governance process and release the energy of change without tearing the structure apart?

Over the past decade, literally hundreds of books and articles have been written on the subject of corporate financial restructuring. Despite this, the word "restructuring" continues to have only symbolic meaning for most people—symbolic of conflict, dislocation, and economic and financial "pain or gain." It is largely perceived in terms of its external consequences for investors, employees, competitors, suppliers, host communities. What the specific consequences are for the corporate entity itself are less well understood. What, precisely, does corporate financial structure mean? What are the key elements of structure, and how do they relate to each other and to financial performance? What do we mean by "financial efficiency," and how is it impacted by structural change? What is the time frame over which changes in efficiency are measured? I address these questions using demonstrated deterioration or improvement in return on investment, not merely in shareholder expectations, as the metric of corporate efficiency.

The decade of the 1980s produced a fundamental and continuing debate over corporate governance. The issue is whether the modern large-scale publicly owned corporation has the capacity for self-discipline to adapt to environmental change in a timely and effective manner. Answering in the negative, some critics are calling for fundamental change in the governance process. At the same time, however, corporate governance in practice shows little change from prior decades.

Reasoning from the standpoint that, in a democratic, free enterprise society, the nation will continue to depend primarily on self-discipline as the means of enforcing socially responsible behavior, I pay particular attention to examples of voluntary restructuring for those characteristics which produced an orderly response to change. These are compared with cases of involuntary restructuring for evidence of similarity and difference in causes and consequences. We will discover, on closer examination, that the similarities are greater than the differences. The nature of change is observed, in fact, to be quite similar. The differences are in the process by which change is accomplished and in the leaders of change, but most important, in the time frame or *pace* of change, which can have profound consequences for the business organization and its various constituencies.

So, judging by this sample of evidence on the performance of corporate America to the test of self-discipline presented by the changed environment of the 1980s, how did we do? As we will see, the answer to that question is decidedly mixed: both reassuring and disappointing. On the negative side, there were cases where, even when the evidence of deteriorating performance was pervasive and persistent, the response of incumbent management was slow and fragmentary. In some instances, any change was strongly resisted, in part owing to the instinct to stay the course and make the established strategy and structure work and in part as an emotional reaction to a challenge to established authority. Even those who voluntarily responded in a vigorous and effective manner were prepared to admit that, with hindsight, it could have been done sooner. Consequently, the stockholder interest, narrowly defined, was not aggressively represented.

On the other hand, no voluntary system of individual response, whether in private enterprise or in the general democratic process, can match the "efficiency" of an arbitrary objective enforced by an absolute authority, which some critics of corporate performance appear to prefer. Despite its legal prerogatives, stockholder interest is only one of several constituent interests whose sustained commitment to a cooperative effort is essential to product-market activity, and it is the responsibility, indeed the imperative, of the chief executive to balance the interests of all constituencies to achieve long-term productivity. This fact of cooperative corporate efficiency, together with the inevitable uncertainties of real-time decision making in an evolving competitive environment, is destined to produce an imperfect result when viewed from a single perspective.

It is natural to speculate—as I do—on the future of corporate evolution and structural change in the 1990s and beyond. The key question is whether the 1980s produced a systemic shift in corporate goals and mission, and in the process by which they are either affected by or insulated from environmental change. Now that we know more clearly what "efficiency," as defined by the capital markets, means, are businesses more likely to pursue that objective more consistently in the future than they did in the past?

The corporate agenda of the 1980s was dominated by the interests of the investors of financial capital, in contrast to the decades of the 1960s and 1970s, when it was dominated by the interests of the investors of human capital: the organizational priorities of career employees. Since the economic function of corporate activity is to produce a superior product or service at a competitive price through the collective commitment of all corporate constituencies, it is apparent that a balance must be struck in the allocation of the corporate value-added among all constituencies.

Historically, human organizations have proved incapable of maintaining a consistent relationship among competing interests and, therefore, a pendulumlike ebb and flow of priorities and payoffs is likely to persist. The question for the 1990s is how long the swing toward the stockholder interest will persist before a countermomentum develops. The study suggests that the priorities which drove the strategy and structure of the 1960s and 1970s are far from dead and may even be reemerging as the forces that propelled the stockholder revolt recede.

But is this the best we can do—to swing from one gut-wrenching restructuring to another from one decade to the next? Can the corporate governance process be improved so as to contribute to a more orderly and efficient adjustment to change? To those who view the problem through the single lens of stockholder priority, the solution appears simple enough: modify the governance process to ensure the absolute priority of the stockholder interest. However, when business enterprise is viewed as a voluntary and cooperative effort among multiple constituencies, the role of an independent professional management team in the balancing of competing interests, as corporate entities evolve from one decade to the next, takes on critical importance.

The Nature of the Evidence

It is important to supply the reader with the nature of the evidence upon which the findings of this study have been based and to explain how it differs from most of the recent academic research on this subject. The corporate restructuring of the 1980s has produced a large volume of academic research centering primarily on its implications for the wealth-creating potential of corporate ownership and on the ability of the shareholder to exert effective discipline on the board of directors and on management. In an effort to provide scientifically demonstrable conclusions, this research has focused almost exclusively on the statistical analysis of large sample studies using broad market data bases.

While this form of research has produced extensive evidence on the links between aggregate corporate behavior and the general capital-market response, it has paid only limited attention to the causes and consequences of restructuring in and for the individual firm and its management. The rationale for individual deviations from the norm is thus largely ignored. To the market as a whole this may be unimportant. To the management of the individual firm it is all-important.

This study brings a different perspective. It seeks to place restructuring in the context of the long-term evolution of an individual enterprise, to understand the organizational process within which fundamental restructuring occurs, and to observe the consequences for the firm and for society. The firm and its management are the unit of analysis. The data are the sequence of decisions and actions by individual firms that affect the management of financial resources taken over extended periods of time. The questions concern the capacity of the internal governance system of the firm to define a strategy and structure responsive to the current corporate environment, which is subject to secular change.

In-depth research on the restructuring process of the individual firm over extended periods of time necessitates the sacrifice of confidence in the generality of the findings in order to achieve confidence in the accuracy and detail of the individual observations. The relatively small and "unscientific" sample on which this study is based was dictated by the time necessary to research each case thoroughly. Within these limits, however, I made every effort to purge the sample of conscious bias in favor of particular conclusions.

I chose as my base of observation companies with the following characteristics:

- They are large, mature, publicly owned corporations that were among the leaders in their chosen product or service industries.
- They represent a broad cross section of industrial activity.
- All underwent major financial restructuring in the 1980s.
- In all cases the restructuring was carried out by management appointed from within the established corporate governance process.
- As a group, they covered the full spectrum of voluntary and involuntary response to change.
- All the companies actively cooperated in the data-gathering process.

The appendix provides a brief profile of the twelve companies used as the research data base. The findings are based not only on all available public information on these companies over the past two or more decades but, also important, on extensive interviews with many of the current and past executives involved in these decisions and actions and, in some cases, with board members. Some internal, nonpublic documentation was also made available. While the findings reflect my views alone, companies cooperating in the study were invited to review the company references for factual accuracy. They were not asked to, nor did they, endorse the findings.

The Organization of the Book

This book is organized around three aspects of structural change. Part I concerns the nature and origins of structural change. A major objective of the research was to explore the historical roots of the structuring process within companies and to explain structure in the context of its evolving environment. It was also concerned with evidence of erosion of the continuing relevance of the structure in place, of the development of an imperative for change, and of the mechanisms by which the impulse for change was triggered. When change occurred, it was important to document the specific nature of the change and its impact on corporate performance. These subjects comprise Part I, and I illustrate them by drawing on the experiences of the companies included in the study.

Part II, on the process of change, focuses exclusively on the detailed experiences of three companies and describes and interprets two decades in the evolution of financial structure in each of three case histories. These were chosen because each illustrates a different stimulus for change: General Mills, where the stimulus originated in the normal process of one generation of management succeeding its predecessor; Burlington Northern, where a timely board intervention introduced new leadership from outside the organization; and CPC International, where a hostile takeover attempt triggered a vigorous and successful counterattack by incumbent management. A sustained focus on one company provides an insight into the process of change that isolated events in multiple settings are unable to provide.

Part III, on the management of change, has three objectives. The first is to characterize the changes in the management of corporate financial resources resulting from the restructuring of the 1980s and to assess the efficiency of a voluntary response to the evolving corporate environment. The second is to consider the prospects for further structural change in the 1990s in the light of the forces that have dominated the formation of corporate financial structure in the preceding decades. The third objective is to draw from this experience ideas that would strengthen the capacity of the modern industrial corporation for effective self-governance and timely renewal.

CHAPTER 2

The Structure of the 1970s:
The Origins of Investor Discontent

Chapter Overview

The sharp acceleration of major financial restructuring that occurred in the 1980s in many of our best-known business corporations commanded widespread public attention. Unfortunately, the media have primarily emphasized the human drama of the power struggle—the personalities and the personal wealth won or lost. Even the more thoughtful academic writings, which have focused on the "market for corporate control," have tended to limit their attention to the near-term consequences for shareholder wealth. Largely missing from these analyses has been the corporate perspective: the forces driving the evolution of corporate priorities, the management process, and the operation of the traditional governance system, which continues to run the vast majority of business enterprises.

One thing is very clear. The events of the 1980s were precipitated in large measure by the common perception among investors that many of the business strategies of the 1960s and 1970s had tipped the balance of corporate priorities in favor of career employees, including professional management. As a result, the wealth of the owners was being dissipated, or so it was increasingly alleged. The sinister phrase "management entrenchment" became popular in academic research, even in schools of business administration—a startling re-

17

minder of how far we had come from the days when the excellence of American professional management was widely proclaimed as a unique competitive advantage.

An aroused investment community sensed that there could be a payoff in the challenge initiated by a new generation of activists, outside the corporate establishment, and supported by allies on Wall Street and lending institutions looking for exceptional returns at limited risk. An increasing number of traditionally passive fund managers were no longer willing to express discontent simply by selling the stock; they began to speak out. We have seen the results.

Why were strategies that appeared to serve these corporations so well in the 1960s and 1970s, and that were generally accepted and even applauded by investors, analysts, and the business press of the time, suddenly so radically wrong for the 1980s? Some observers believe that the answer lies in gross mismanagement by an all-powerful and self-serving group of professional managers acting with the tacit approval of a negligent board of directors. In an article entitled "The Eclipse of the Public Corporation," Michael Jensen has written:

The public corporation is a social invention of vast historical importance. Its genius is rooted in its capacity to spread financial risk over the diversified portfolios of millions of individuals and institutions and to allow investors to customize risk to their unique circumstances and predilections . . .

From the beginning, though, these risk-bearing benefits came at a cost. Tradable ownership claims create fundamental conflicts of interest between those who bear risk (the shareholders) and those who manage risk (the executives) . . .

The idea that outside directors with little or no equity stake in the company could effectively monitor and discipline the managers who selected them has proven hollow at best. In practice, only the capital markets have played much of a control function—and for a long time they were hampered by legal constraints . . .

Takeovers and buyouts both create new value and unlock value destroyed by management through misguided policies. I estimate that transactions associated with the market for corporate control unlocked shareholder gains (in target companies alone) of more than $500 billion between 1977 and 1988—more than 50% of the cash dividends paid by the entire corporate sector over this same period.

The widespread waste and inefficiency of the public corporation and its inability to adapt to changing economic circumstances have generated a wave of organizational innovation over the last 15 years—innovation driven by the rebirth of "active investors."[1]

Certainly self-interest is a part of the motivation of most, if not all, managers, as it is in other walks of life. However, the strategy and actions of large publicly owned corporations cannot be sustained merely to serve the will of incumbent chief executives. They must also serve the self-interest of some or all of the major constituencies that voluntarily cooperate to produce a profitable product or service: employees, unions, suppliers, customers, shareholders, and host communities. Thus, to understand the restructuring of the 1980s we must understand the economic rationale behind the structure of the 1960s and 1970s, which explains the motivations of managements and the interests served and why they prevailed so broadly and so long.

This chapter begins by placing the reader at a conference of the senior management of a major consumer-goods corporation in 1968, listening to the chief executive's keynote address. What comes through is typical of the management mind-set of the time: an introverted, corporate view of the business mission focused on growth, diversification, and opportunity for the "corporate family." To a 1980s ear, reference to the stockholder interest is strangely absent, and there is even a renunciation of "purely economic" goals.

Who were these men leading corporate enterprises in the 1960s and 1970s? The chapter reminds us that they were the children of the Great Depression who, through their own experience or that of their parents, had learned to be wary of dependence on fickle capital markets and unreliable institutional relationships—to be independent, self-reliant, and self-sufficient both in personal and in corporate life.

It was a period when the social and legal climate encouraged management to adopt a pluralistic view of their responsibility to the various corporate constituencies. As career employees themselves, it was natural for management to identify with all constituents who were long-term investors in the enterprise and to view shareholders in the same light. "Loyalty" was the key word—commitment to the success of an enterprise within which each constituent found economic and social fulfillment.

But shareholders were increasingly looking beyond the individual corporate entity to find greater investment potential and greater

[1]Michael C. Jensen, "Eclipse of the Public Corporation," *Harvard Business Review*, vol. 67, no. 5, September–October 1989, pp. 61–74.

safety of principal with the help of a new generation of fund managers who were investing in the securities of the market as a whole. New investment opportunity meant that shareholders no longer identified with individual entities but with a broad corporate portfolio. To corporate leadership, stockholders—or those who represented them— were increasingly diversified and mobile—and therefore, by definition, "disloyal"—just at the time when other constituents—notably career jobholders—were increasingly undiversified and immobile. This was significantly affected by, among other things, the two-income family anchored to a single geographic location.

There were several points of departure between the interests of diversified investors of financial capital and undiversified investors of human capital. The locus of opportunity was one. To shareholders, risk reduction and growth potential were best achieved in the market as a whole; to career employees, the corporation was their universe of opportunity. The accumulation of reserves was another. The solvency and security of the corporate entity was enhanced by conservative financial policies: redundant assets and excess debt capacity. To the diversified investor, such policies appeared as underutilized resources that should be released to shareholders for investment elsewhere. A third point of departure was unexploited trade-offs in the management of funds flows which, if actively pursued, would result in a redistribution of the corporate value-added to shareholders and away from other constituencies.

Typically, this divergence of interest did not manifest itself suddenly but grew over time, obscured by the ebb and flow of events. It tended to emerge in time of crisis when a sudden change of fortune focused attention on the causes and consequence for each constituency and on their relative gains or losses. The chapter ends with the illustration of the 1960s and 1970s era in the experience of one company, Armco. The problems which had been latent in the corporate and financial strategy of the 1970s suddenly surfaced in 1982 with a collapse of earnings and cash flows so severe that the company spent the next decade struggling to survive. Though an extreme case, it highlights the characteristics of the 1970s epitomized by the chapter subtitle, "The Origins of Investor Discontent."

The 1970s

To illuminate the mind-set of the management of the time, we revisit a conference held in 1968 at which the chief executive of a major consumer-goods corporation addressed an audience of his top managers. All segments of the company's worldwide operations were represented, and the event was an important consensus-building opportunity. The CEO's keynote address said, in part:

Welcome to the International Strategic Planning conference, to a meeting which will have been a total failure if any of you leave here unconcerned, uncommitted, unresolved to change your company for the better. Seven years ago we met right here; actually in this very room . . . You will recall we talked a great deal about change . . . The past seven years have seen many changes . . . Overall, the changes of the past seven years have been highly constructive. But paradoxically, the most constructive change of all may well have been the destruction of an attitude that the future takes care of itself. Circumstances—our own and those in the world around us—have forced us to recognize the inevitability of change . . .

A year ago we announced to the whole wide world that our goals were to double sales and double earnings in ten years. Public announcements on our goals put us in the position of making a commitment. And this is exactly what we intended . . . We cannot reach our goal simply by doing what we have been doing, no matter how well we do it . . . This means we must add new business through development and acquisition. And it means that a significant portion of what we add must be substantially different from our existing business . . . I would propose that we increase our participation in several industries in which we now have only a slim foothold, or none at all . . .

Although planning our changing future is the primary purpose of this meeting, we have an important secondary purpose as well . . . Our purpose is to make sure that this new approach to management is fully understood by you who are the managers . . . The majority of our decisions are in one of six identifiable units, each standing pretty much apart, each with a discrete business of its own, each reasonably autonomous and self-sufficient . . . in other words, each a major profit center . . . And of course there is nothing sacred about the number six. Some day the number should be seven, eight, ten, or more . . .

Since our corporate resources are not unlimited, as is true of any company, we have to be selective in these investments, must decide which investments must be assigned highest priority, which offer the best return on investment. The corporation must pursue business opportunities which do not logically fit within even the broad definitions of our present six existing major profit centers . . .

When it comes to setting the corporate direction, deciding who we are and what we want to become, it may seem rather unsatisfactory to you that the corporation provides no ringing, Olympian answer . . . To you more disturbing still may be the apparent failure to come up with a corporate mission, which will stir our hearts and unite us in common purpose, as they say. I don't mean to joke at these rather grandly worded statements. All of us, all of you, who are experienced in business appreciate that beyond a point . . . we are not purely economic beings. We reach out for a sense of mission which will strengthen our membership in the human race as well as in its corporate chapter. It is true that the corporate goals . . . are phrased in financial terms. But I urge you to look beyond these terms and beyond the abstraction of a corporation . . . and direct your gaze to the business in which we are engaged. There you will find not one but a great number and variety of missions, all of them meaningful, all of them real and not abstract, and each of them growing directly out of the operation of a particular business . . . All of them produce goods and services of proven utility and benefit to the ultimate consumer . . . It is fair to say that the contribution of these businesses is far, far greater than their purely financial increment. These companies are much more than just economic instruments. And so, as long as you continue to respond to these opportunities which represent the fulfillment of human needs, you and your associates can be proud of the enterprises which you operate. This is your mission and it is real and quite clear.

Leadership in the 1970s:
Motivation and Rationale

The International Strategic Planning address contains several points that reflect management thinking of the 1960s and 1970s. The reader should bear in mind that the corporate leaders of the time were mostly men who had served their early business apprenticeship in a period dominated by economic stress, uncertainty, and disruption. They had come of age during the Great Depression of the 1930s—the collapse of the stock market, near collapse of the banking system, massive regulation of all major financial institutions, and widespread personal and corporate bankruptcy. The 1940s brought World War II and military service, which disrupted both corporate and personal lives. The late 1940s and 1950s were a period when both corporations and businessmen and -women were putting their lives and careers back into what they hoped would be a new sense of order and progress.

Individual and corporate survival and continuity were persistent concerns. There was a deep distrust of the nation's financial institutions and of the markets for debt and equity. Conservative by nature and occupation, these corporate leaders were self-sufficient, shunned unnecessary financial risk, and welcomed access to assured reserves. Hence, given the opportunity to set the goals and standards for a major enterprise, they made their own personal convictions and values part and parcel of the corporate ethic.

Representative of its time, the plan for the 1970s cited in the previous section outlined the following key elements:

1. Proactive change is essential and inevitable.
2. The company has made a bold commitment to sustained growth, including growth by acquisition.
3. Such growth will require a move into areas hitherto unknown to the company.
4. The resulting corporate family will be composed of as many as 10 or more discrete and self-sufficient profit centers.
5. Operating control will be delegated to those best able to run each business unit. Corporate headquarters will be concerned primarily with allocating scarce resources across the enterprise for maximum aggregate return on investment.
6. A human organization demands a powerful sense of community and mission in order to develop a strong and consistent thrust. This is not to be found in "purely economic" goals. To quote again: "It is true that the corporate goals . . . are phrased in financial terms. But I urge you to look beyond these terms . . . [to the] fulfillment of human needs . . . You and your associates can be proud of the enterprises which you operate. This is your mission."

Twenty-five years have passed since the CEO spoke, and the rationale behind his words is alien to the financial environment of the early 1990s with its single-minded allegiance to the creation of shareholder wealth. In my view, the essence of the corporate mission of this and many other companies of that day was the concept of the individual corporation as an independent and self-sustaining economic and financial entity within which all primary constituent interests, including shareholders, could fulfill their economic objectives. Growth, diversification, and a high degree of independence from the public capital markets were essential ingredients of long-term economic self-sufficiency.

A review of internal planning documents of the time clearly indicates how widespread the concept of multiconstituent responsibility had become among large publicly owned U.S. corporations.[2] Statements of the corporate mission that prefaced the detailed strategic plan customarily cited the responsibility of serving the interests of customers, employees, stockholders, and the society at large, collectively. In contrast to the chairman's traditional pledge of allegiance to shareholders in the annual report, the stockholder interest was rarely mentioned as a priority in memoranda to the rank and file of management (note the total absence of reference to stockholder interest in the International Strategic Planning address).

Occasionally the issue surfaced in public discussion. In an article published in 1959, the dean of the Yale Law School, Eugene Rostow, joined the ongoing debate by weighing in on behalf of the primacy of stockholder property rights. He took exception to a statement by the then chairman of the Standard Oil Company of New Jersey, who had asserted that the managers of his company conduct its affairs "in such a way as to maintain an equitable and working balance among the claims of the various directly interested groups—stockholders, employees, customers and the public at large."[3]

On the other side of the debate was no less a person than Mr. Justice William O. Douglas who, while chairman of the Securities and Exchange Commission, had stated: "Today it is generally recognized that all corporations possess an element of public interest. A corporation director must think not only of the stockholder but also of the laborer, the supplier, the purchaser and the ultimate consumer."[4] The chief executive, whose accustomed pragmatism led him to plan with multiple constituencies in mind, was in tune with a broad segment of public thought.

Career Jobholder/Transient Stockholder

One way to view the fundamental shift in corporate financial structuring from the 1960s and 1970s to the 1980s—admittedly somewhat oversimplified—is to see it as a shift in the center of power from the immobile jobholder to the increasingly transient stockholder.

---

[2] See Gordon Donaldson and Jay W. Lorsch, *Decision Making at the Top* (New York: Basic Books, 1983).

[3] Edward S. Mason, ed., *The Corporation in Modern Society* (Cambridge, Mass.: Harvard University Press, 1959), p. 60.

[4] Ibid., p. 6.

Jobholders at all levels have traditionally looked to the individual corporation as the source of their lifetime economic welfare. It was an expectation to be encouraged, since an unconditional commitment from the work force served the best interest of corporate leadership.

This commitment was reinforced by the increasing importance of pension plans and other nonportable fringe benefits in the total compensation package. Most dependent and most vulnerable were people in midcareer with children attending increasingly expensive schools. And while wives had once moved dutifully wherever their husbands were posted, dual careers now tied families to one location. The jobholder was increasingly undiversified and immobile.

In contrast, shareholders were moving in the opposite direction at an accelerating pace. In the 1960s, chief executives could still legitimately lay claim to a substantial body of "loyal" stockholders whose equity holdings consisted of a small number of personally selected corporations in which they invested for the long term. These were the folks to whom the annual report could be dedicated with reciprocal and heartfelt loyalty since they represented an equity interest identical to that of senior management—undiversified and immobile.

However, the race was on among a new breed of mutual fund managers to win the minds, if not the hearts, of the public investor to a new concept of wealth maximization and risk minimization in the diversified portfolio. By the early 1970s, investment institutions (mutual and pension funds) generally held a large and growing fraction of the equities of major public corporations. The portfolio manager was a radically different shareholder from the dedicated individual shareholder. Drawing on the enormous potential of a broad, deep, and relatively efficient national and international capital market, the portfolio manager moved resources freely across the full range of corporate equities, loyal only to the goal of improving portfolio performance. The typical shareholder in the 1970s and 1980s was, unlike the typical jobholder, highly mobile and highly diversified. The stage was set for an issue on which their interests sharply diverged.

Management was slow to adjust to the new ownership priorities, not because corporate leaders were unaware of the market trends, but because they were themselves, through their jobs, stock ownership, and stock options, intensely loyal investors in single companies. Admittedly, stock ownership should focus management attention on opportunities to enhance equity values and thereby increase personal wealth. But the larger game—that of corporate leadership—would rule out many of the value-enhancing options exercised in the 1980s, which were in conflict with corporate, as opposed to shareholder, priorities. Management naturally preferred to cherish the image of a dedicated individual shareholder because it was consistent with those corporate goals which career management preferred—goals centered on individual corporate continuity and growth.

Financial economists often wonder why growth is so central to management thinking. For the career jobholder the answer is obvious. First, growth and share of market are central to most product-market strategies, keeping pace at least with the growth rate of primary demand in the industry and demonstrating competitive superiority by gaining share on one's closest rivals. Growth is also the environment that best promotes employment opportunity, improved compensation, and upward mobility. It is a more exciting environment in which to work. Finally, a growth environment is an easier setting in which to manage: more resources, more room to negotiate, easier to mask or excuse mistakes.

By contrast, to the highly mobile and diversified portfolio manager it is the growth rate of the economy as a whole, or sectors of the economy, that is important, not that of any one company. It is the *quality* of the earnings of the individual company that matters, not quantity. If smaller means a better return on investment, then small is beautiful. If loyalty means holding resources captive to inferior rates of return, then loyalty is a bad word. There is little concern for the growth or even the survival of the individual firm—only that, if survival is in question, the investor accurately forecasts the outcome. It is not surprising that the individual chief executive found this to be heresy.

There is a similar divergence of views regarding diversification. At certain stages of industry and company history, diversification is essential to the preservation of management careers and to corporate survival. When product markets mature and rates of return begin to erode, it is inevitable that the corporation will search for new sources of revenue and growth potential. "Growth" and "stability" are the two words most commonly used to justify diversification. In the late 1960s, James McFarland, chief executive of General Mills, launched an era of aggressive diversification and coined the phrase "The All-Weather Growth Company," a term designed to capture the unqualified commitment of both jobholders and stockholders.

For the jobholder it was an easier sell. One more leg on the corporate stool, as it was sometimes described, made job potential, particularly at upper levels, more secure and exciting. If the corporation was viewed as a portfolio, then growing markets could pick up the slack from mature markets in performance and resource utilization. When one market was down another would, it was hoped, be up. Thus a new base of earnings would ensure the long-term survival of the corporate entity. In keeping with the corporate portfolio concept, many corporate names were changed to a more universal image: Corn Products to CPC International, Household Finance to Household International, Armco Steel to Armco Inc., Sun Oil to the Sun Company.

At a more personal level, a motive for diversification in a company struggling to cope with the problems of corporate old age is weariness and boredom on the part of management. In private conversations, top managers admit to becoming worn down by another round with the same intractable problems. Diversification offers the prospect of new and exciting frontiers. One can only speculate as to how far personal considerations rather than corporate priorities influenced these decisions.

A third central management concern of the time, self-sufficiency, also pitted jobholder against stockholder. I have noted how post-depression, postwar managers were unwilling to trust the availability of resources critical to the future of the enterprise to an unpredictable place in the queue at the capital-market window, where timing was all-important. Career jobholders particularly benefit from an internal capital market with reserves on which to draw in time of emergency, and are unaware and unaffected by any financial sacrifice this places on equity investors.

Financial investors, on the other hand—particularly diversified ones—would prefer that the firm be dependent on explicit and regular capital-market approval for major new investment decisions. The risk that a key strategic action might be delayed or aborted by the capital-market process, which looms large to the individual CEO and the individual company, is inconsequential to the diversified portfolio holder.

Thus the central precepts that governed the corporate financial structure of the 1960s and 1970s had a clear, if unconscious, bias in favor of the investors of human capital. In defense of the managements of the time, it is not at all clear that they saw the trade-offs, so convinced were they that the corporate self-interest, and therefore the presumed self-interest of all constituencies, was being served.

And, as we shall see later, the signals from the capital market regarding the strategies of the 1970s were, on the whole, supportive of management.

The Social Environment

This book makes no pretense at documenting the direct influence of the political, fiscal, and regulatory environment of the 1960s and 1970s on the development of the corporate strategies of growth, diversification, and self-sufficiency. It is apparent, however, that, to management, the corporate environment of the time represented a powerful social endorsement of its corporate strategies.

Most of the companies included in this study were not only large but were also market leaders. It is an axiom of competition that as share of market increases it becomes increasingly difficult to make further inroads on competitors' entrenched positions. Thus the rate of growth of the mature market leader tends to drift down toward the rate of growth of the industry as a whole.

In the United States a major factor accelerating this trend during the post–World War II era was the active intervention of the federal government through regulation and antitrust action. It was apparent that for these companies, further penetration into competitors' market share, particularly by acquisition, could invoke legal action that at best would involve costly delays and at worst abort the intended expansion. As a result, leading companies, particularly in mature industries, turned to unrelated diversification at home and to expansion abroad as the means of maintaining a vigorous and "hassle-free" growth environment within the company. This would have happened anyway—even a total monopolist in a mature industry must find a way to escape stagnation. But the social endorsement of vigorous competition accelerated the trend.

The pattern of funding for growth and diversification was also strongly influenced by the intended and unintended regulatory and fiscal policies of the federal government. I have already noted management's preference for financial self-sufficiency. In particular this meant the virtual exclusion of the unreliable equity markets as a source of ongoing cash requirements. This was motivated for two primary reasons. The key index of equity performance at the time was earnings per share (EPS); an increase in the number of shares, in advance of the profitable investment of the funds provided, was a sure way to slow the growth of EPS. In contrast, shares issued for the purchase of a newly acquired subsidiary or industry partner brought an immediate and usually fully offsetting increase in earnings.

The second reason to avoid new equity issues for cash was the active involvement of the government through the Securities and Exchange Commission oversight process. Designed to protect unwary investors from abuse by incompetent or unscrupulous corporate managers, it focused an uncomfortable public spotlight on a firm's investment program at a time when it might prefer anonymity. More important, the process imposed a lengthy review process of uncertain duration when timing of an issue was absolutely critical. In contrast, corporate requirements demanded access to the external equity market when the funds were needed and at a price that justified the investment. If the needed equity funds could be obtained internally, even at some delay, the planning process could be more reliable.

Happily for management, the internal equity capital market (retained earnings) was encouraged and justified in shareholders' eyes by the tax policies of the federal government. The fact that most shareholders are in upper-income brackets and that tax rates favor capital gains over ordinary income—dividends—leads to a preference for earnings retention and reinvestment over dividend distribution. One can, of course, imagine circumstances where, even with the tax differential, it might be better for shareholders to invest dividends elsewhere than to recommit earnings to perpetuate inferior returns in a weak or declining industry. However, management, with its accustomed optimism about the latest strategic plan to rejuvenate earnings, would make no such assumption.

Overall, society appeared to endorse the investment and funding policies of the 1970s that were also in the corporate self-interest.

The Voice of the Capital Markets

If, as suggested previously, a management preoccupation with growth for growth's sake, unrelated diversification, and independence from the direct discipline of the capital markets was harming investor interests during the 1970s, why was there no outcry? There were several reasons.

One was the traditional passivity of the public shareholder who, with access to a well-organized capital market, minimized the cost of real or perceived mismanagement by the quick and certain process of selling the stock rather than by the long and highly uncertain process of attempting to change management behavior. Proxy votes and the archaic ritual of the shareholders' meeting had no real power. Similarly, the growing number of potentially influential portfolio managers who were judged by year-to-year performance found selling the stock the only practical way to maximize return or to minimize the cost of investment error. There were no natural champions of the stockholder interest who would or could take on corporate leadership. The financial backing and incentive structure were not yet in place.

In the early days of these companies, there was usually a concentrated block of equity in the hands of the founders or their heirs. So a distinctive and influential equity constituency was represented. As these concentrations dispersed, management began to listen with some care to the professional security analyst and, to a lesser extent, the business press. This was particularly true of industry analysts who had built a reputation for astute interpretation of industry and company trends. Of course, management's natural tendency is to welcome favorable reports and screen out unfavorable ones, but it is hard to ignore persistent criticism from acknowledged industry experts.

However, from the viewpoint of an objective market discipline, there was a potentially fatal flaw inherent in the job analysts were assigned to do. Like individual corporate managers, they had a major long-term investment in intimate knowledge of particular industries and particular companies. A solid relationship with management was an important avenue of information. Their recommendations to buy, sell, or hold related to particular stocks of particular companies, not to portfolios. Their standard of comparison was, like management's, primarily the company's own past performance and its principal industry competitors.

In these respects, most of the companies in this study did well in the 1970s. They showed regular improvement and at least held their own in their industry. After all, if the number of shares was not growing and total earnings were, however slowly, earnings per share would show a positive upward trend. In a generally buoyant economy, this was to be expected: a rising tide raises all boats. As a result, the firms received their fair share of positive recommendations from industry analysts. A study of analysts' reports and the business press of that time fails to reveal widespread or persistent criticism of general corporate strategy, and certainly no consensus.

The basic problem of the period was one common to most firms—a gradual and, at the time, imperceptible drift in the focus of the management of resources that was eroding equity returns. It was what economists would call the opportunity cost of underutilized resources—mismatched product lines lacking real synergy and critical mass, and organizational and operational slack from which constituencies other than shareholders largely benefited. With hindsight, the trends were strikingly clear; looking forward from the early 1970s, they were not.

A Case in Point: Armco Steel

Armco Steel was founded in 1900 by George M. Verity, in Middletown, Ohio, as the American Rolling Mill Company. By the beginning of the post–World War II era it had become, through internal growth, merger, and acquisition, one of the largest integrated steel companies in the United States. Vertical integration—backward to the sources of raw materials and forward to fabricated steel products—had always been central to corporate strategy. In recognition of this, in 1948 the company changed its name to Armco Steel.

While a deep-seated and vigorous steelmaking culture permeated the company from its founding, dissatisfaction with the fundamental economic and financial characteristics of the markets for basic steel output in the United States began to surface in public discussion by Armco's management. The strong demand for steel, which came in the aftermath of World War II as countries sought to rebuild their domestic infrastructure and industrial capacity, came to an end in the late 1950s. It was replaced by a sustained secular decline, punctuated by the periodic swings in demand and profitability characteristic of a durable-goods industry. Several factors combined to produce a stagnant industry: the development of substitute materials (aluminum, plastic, and glass), changing technology, which favored dispersed rather than concentrated steel production, aggressive foreign competition, labor unrest, and public mistrust of "big steel" in times of crisis. One Armco executive of the time gloomily described steel as a dying industry.

As management reviewed its options, the organizational imperative for growth potential, year-to-year stability and continuity, and enhanced profitability became dominant themes. Since none of the imperatives appeared attainable in the foreseeable environment of the American steel industry, management inevitably began to look outside its industry for new corporate opportunity. The seeds of Armco's diversification strategy had actually been sown in the 1950s, seeds which, in the time of harvest—the 1980s—would prove to be the tares in the wheat. In particular, two diversification decisions taken in the 1950s set the stage for the corporate strategy of the next two decades, and the subsequent convulsive restructuring of the 1980s.

One of these was the acquisition of the National Supply Company, supplier and manufacturer of oil field machinery and equipment, in 1958. In response to this announcement, *Iron Age* wrote, approvingly: "Armco is diversified, but it is one of the few major mills without a tubular line. National Supply offered a natural answer to the problem." It appeared to be a competition-induced piece of forward integration. By the 1970s, industrial products and services, of which National Supply was a key component, accounted for one-fifth of Armco's gross revenues.

A second, much more controversial—and ultimately disastrous—diversification was Armco's move into financial services. What was a steel company doing in financial services? Undoubtedly the appeal was that of an apparently self-funding growth industry with unusual profit potential, a cyclical pattern to earnings that would run counter to the steel industry, and none of the intractable problems of steel. This diversification began innocently enough as the brainchild of Armco financial managers seeking to cut corporate insurance costs through self-insurance via a captive subsidiary called Bellefonte. The move proved successful, so it was inevitable that its managers would ask, Why not insure other firms as well? and answered in the vigorous affirmative, as we shall see later.

Through the 1960s Armco's corporate and financial performance continued to be determined by the fortunes of steel. That performance reinforced the notion that corporate goals had to be sought outside the industry. Gross revenues grew at a modest rate of 6% per annum and return on sales was trending downward, as was the return on equity—only 5.4% in 1970. In 1965, C. William Verity, Jr., grandson of the founder, had become president and CEO of Armco at the age of 49. (His father had served as executive vice president.) It was Verity whose vision shaped the plan for Armco's corporate renewal through the late 1960s and the 1970s. Looking back from the vantage point of 1980, *Nation's Business* characterized Verity as "The Maverick Who Made Armco Stronger than Steel." Later events would prove this assessment seriously in error.

Verity's long-range strategic plan involved a three-pronged attack: (1) a major modernization of steelmaking facilities to increase efficiency and reduce costs; (2) increased emphasis on higher-margin specialty steel and related materials; and (3) decreased dependence on steel through further diversification. A major surge of investments in steelmaking facilities occurred in 1965–1971 and again in 1975–1976. HITCO, a manufacturer of high-performance nonmetallic materials, was acquired in 1969. In 1970, the company was calling itself an International Materials Company.

Most important, from the viewpoint of later restructuring, diversification received a new and powerful impetus. In 1966, Verity, believing that Armco's entry into new fields was the fastest way for the company to grow, appointed the Strategic Planning Task Force. The clearest evidence of the willingness to reach well beyond traditional experience was the formation early in 1969 of a new subsidiary to lease major capital equipment: industrial machinery such as drilling rigs, jet aircraft, ships, and railroad rolling stock. The move was motivated by a perceived opportunity to utilize Armco's substantial financial resources at superior rates of return. The first-year target was to invest $150 million in the enterprise.

Continuing this trend, Armco, in 1969, formed a financial enterprises group as a separate profit center. In addition to leasing, the insurance business was to be greatly expanded, and the company began to explore real estate development as a new growth opportunity. In 1972, diversification was given added incentive by the split of the corporate organization into two operating groups: the Steel Group and the Enterprises Group. The head of the Enterprises Group was one of two executive vice presidents, D.C. Boone. Boone had been corporate controller until 1969, when he became senior vice president, finance. The Enterprises Group had a distinctive financial services flavor.

Diversification continued through the 1970s. In 1976, Armco announced a long-range plan of redeployment of assets over the next nine years, as follows:

	1976	1985
Oil field equipment & services	8%	12%
Metal products	8%	12%
Specialty steel	10%	13%
Mining	6%	9%
Industrial products & services	2%	5%
Financial services	3%	11%
Carbon steel	63%	38%

In a 1978 update of the plan, Verity announced that by that date 40% of Armco's assets were employed outside the steel industry: "That means Armco will become less and less a steel manufacturer, and more and more a diversified company." In line with this, the shareholders were asked at the April annual meeting to change the company name from Armco Steel Corporation to Armco Inc.

There was general agreement among observers that Armco's diversification program through the 1970s had strongly supported Armco financial performance and distinguished it from other steel companies. Typical of the business press of the period, an article in *Business Week* of December 1977, titled "Diversification That Offsets the Slack in Steel," reported that Armco had outperformed the top steelmakers in the late 1970s. From 1973 to 1979, the contribution of steel mill products to operating profit had declined from 69% to 23%. The slack was taken up in major part by revenues from oil field equipment, financial services, and fabricated products.

Through the 1970s, Armco's Bellefonte insurance company had pursued an aggressive growth policy in property and casualty insurance. The rapid rise in premium income was achieved by the company's assuming a level of risk that few other major insurers would accept. The business press reported that Armco was insuring, among other things, the Libyan navy under the notorious Colonel Muammar Khadafy. Problems inherent in aggressive growth first surfaced in 1975, when claims exceeded income, requiring the first of a series of capital infusions. They persisted and, in 1979, A.M. Best reduced Bellefonte's insurance rating from A to B. A shake-up in Bellefonte management followed, resulting in the hiring of new outside leadership. The consequence was a decision to outgrow the problem through the acquisition of Northwestern National Insurance Company (1980), thereby doubling the size of the insurance operation and adding a more diversified risk portfolio as well as a new layer of industry expertise.

As the decade came to a close, Verity, who had become increasingly involved in political affairs in Washington, resigned as CEO, continuing as chairman of the board until 1982. Despite the growing importance of the nonsteel components of the Armco revenue stream, he chose as his successor Harry Holliday, a veteran Armco steel man with no experience in the emerging nonsteel businesses. It was, however, a decision designed to ensure the continuance of the strategic mandate then in place for over a decade.

The Legacy of the 1970s

No single company case history can capture the full range of the nation's corporate agenda during this or any other pivotal period. However, Armco illustrates the dominant management philosophy that motivated corporate goals and strategy during the decade, leading to an unsustainable tension among corporate constituencies and erupting in the restructuring frenzy of the 1980s.

For Armco, this philosophy was based on the following, apparently self-evident, propositions:

- that one company could provide the optimal set of investment opportunities to satisfy the needs and interests of all constituent groups;
- that sustained organizational growth was a precondition of organizational well-being;
- that if growth could not be sustained within traditional product markets, it should be pursued among the best of whatever alternative opportunities were accessible by the company at the time;
- that diversification, however unrelated to primary product markets, would promote growth, reduce risk, and increase profitability;
- that the cornerstone of corporate financial independence was a conservative debt policy—in Armco's case measured by an A or better bond rating.

How well did Armco do, judged by its own standards?

- Its gross revenues grew from $1.6 billion in 1969 to $5.0 billion in 1979.
- It diversified significantly, as we have seen.
- Company earnings, it was generally agreed, were more stable than those of the steel industry as a whole, thanks to diversification.
- The debt-equity ratio declined from a high in 1970 of .55 to a low in 1980 of .28, and corporate liquidity (cash balances plus unused debt capacity) increased substantially and continuously during the period. The bond rating was apparently secure.

However, the achievement of specific financial goals over the decade was modest at best. Three goals were persistently stated:

(1) growth in earnings per share, (2) regular and increasing cash dividends, and (3) return on book equity (ROE) approaching 17%. With regard to earnings per share, it must be noted that for a company which consistently reinvests 50% or more of its earnings, as Armco did, it should not be difficult to raise the absolute amount of earnings per share. Nevertheless, Armco could not escape the drag of its basic steel component, and it took a decade to raise EPS from $3.01 to $4.88, an average annual increase of only 6%.

Of more direct relevance was the return on shareholders' invested capital (book equity). During the last five years of this decade (1975–1979), ROE ranged between 8.4% and 13.4%. During the same period, U.S. Treasury bills earned close to 6%, risk free. There were clearly better risk-equivalent investment alternatives available in the capital markets.

Despite this, however, Verity could look back on his term of stewardship and point to the fact that, on a relative basis, Armco had outperformed the market. During the period 1965–1979, the value of Armco stock grew at an annual rate of 4%, compared to negative 2% for the steel industry as a whole and a positive 2.5% for the Standard & Poor's (S&P) 500 index. Investors apparently approved of the direction in which he had taken the company.

On the other hand, taking the equity market as a whole, there was growing evidence throughout the 1970s of investor dissatisfaction with the direction of the nation's corporate goals and priorities. This is most clearly and objectively apparent in Figures 2.1 and 2.2. They show the ratio of equity prices to the two basic indices of corporate performance—accumulated investment (at book value) and earnings. Generally, the more confident investors are in management performance, the more aggressive the bidding for available equities and the higher the price per unit of earnings or invested capital. In contrast, these figures clearly show a distinct and persistent downward trend in the ratios during the decade. Clearly, investors were willing to pay substantially less for a dollar of investment or a dollar of earnings at the end of the decade than they had at the beginning. This was true for Armco, for the steel industry, and for the market as a whole. Management was having to run faster and faster to stay in place. Note also the depressing fact that for Armco and the steel industry, each new dollar of earnings retained and reinvested in the business was being valued by the market at around 50 cents.

Later events would demonstrate the legacy of the 1970s, about which the capital markets were reflecting increasing concern:

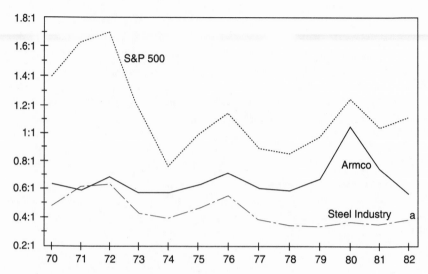

Figure 2.1   Armco Market-Price to Book-Value Ratio

[a]Steel industry: Inland, Wheeling, and Bethlehem Steel averages.
Source: Standard & Poor's COMPUSTAT.

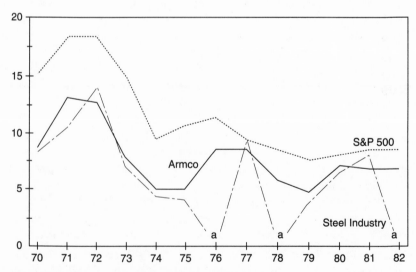

Figure 2.2   Armco Price-Earnings Ratio

[a]Industry earnings negative in 1976, 1978, and 1982—no meaningful data point.
Source: Standard & Poor's COMPUSTAT.

- Corporate investment was divided into isolated pockets of limited investment opportunity, and equity capital was being held captive to whatever returns the available corporate options could produce.
- The unrelenting pursuit of growth led some companies to seek opportunistic diversification with little regard for their established experience or market power to realize superior competitive return on investment.
- With corporate organizational priorities dominant, financial slack had developed in the system, which suggested opportunities to enhance returns merely by tougher management controls.
- The growing levels of corporate liquidity resulting from years of conservative financing policy were an invitation to some to attempt the purchase of companies with their own money.

A Time of Reckoning

We have seen these features illustrated in greater or lesser degree in the Armco story. There were, in addition, some unique aspects of the specific paths Armco had chosen to follow, which were to prove almost fatal, and Harry Holliday, the new CEO, was the unhappy victim of this inheritance. Following the lead set by Verity, now his board chairman, Holliday aggressively continued the pursuit of growth in energy-related equipment, financial services, and steel. In 1981, Holliday declared a "new dawn for steel" (every new day brings a new dawn, it seems) and launched a major new capital-expenditure program in basic steel productive facilities.

Then, in 1982, the bottom fell out for Armco. For the first time in 44 years, Armco suddenly reported a huge loss: $345 million, compared to a profit of $294 million in 1981. Even worse, cash flows were sharply negative, producing a wide range of near-panic responses: in one year, a 23% reduction in the work force, a 50% reduction in spending, $500 million in assets that "no longer fit our strategic plan" up for sale, a 55% cut in the quarterly cash dividend rate.

The general economic recession of 1982 had once again demonstrated the cyclicality of steel, but more ominous were that (1) the collapse of the OPEC–created boom in the American oil patch vividly demonstrated that the intended risk-reducing diversification into oil field machinery and equipment had a violent cycle of its own, which could, and did, coincide with that of steel and (2) the foray into

insurance had led the top management of Armco unknowingly into an accumulation of high-risk exposure, which its management of financial services had been able to mask as long—but only as long—as rapid growth could be maintained. All three: steel, energy, and financial services collapsed at once. It was the beginning of a drastic restructuring process that has continued to this day and has seen the piece-by-piece dismantling of Verity's plan for the 1970s.

Despite these ominous signs, Holliday put up a brave and reassuring front:

Our overall 1982 results came from the fact that not one of the major economic sectors corresponding to our six separate lines of business had a decent year. This doesn't happen very often. We do not believe it will continue to be this bad, on this broad front, for long. We will continue our strategy of concentrating on these six separate segments . . . The current slump has slowed our timetable for reaching the diversity and size we want. But we fully expect to reach those goals.[5]

When Holliday first came under attack, his instinctive response was to reaffirm that the strategy which had worked so well in the 1970s was still firmly in place.

The leadership of a large, diverse, and dispersed organization is an immensely challenging assignment. To articulate a clear and consistent set of goals, to develop an effective and coherent strategy for the achievement of those goals, and particularly to gain and maintain companywide consensus and commitment to achievement, requires exceptional energy and managerial ability. Once in motion, the chosen course of action takes on a force of its own, the forward momentum of which is, like a supertanker, most difficult to deflect. It takes a massive counterforce to produce radical change in direction—or to avoid a destructive collision.

For Armco it was the event of sudden, large, and unexpected losses and life-threatening, persistent cash flow deficits that had such an effect. For other companies, other imperatives prevailed. The next chapter will examine the imperative for change across a diverse spectrum of companies which underwent major restructuring in the 1980s. It presents the results of a search for the common forces that precipitated radical change on a massive scale during this unique period in U.S. corporate history.

[5] Armco, *Annual Report*, 1982.

CHAPTER 3

The Imperative for Change

Chapter Overview

The 1980s yielded many examples of financial restructuring under the pressure of a direct challenge to the authority of incumbent management. Under threat of a hostile bid for control, the imperative for change is obvious: do what has to be done to retain the confidence of the constituency represented by the challenger. Some of these responses were in the first instance purely defensive, but even if successful in fending off the attackers, they were usually followed by genuine restructuring designed to address lingering problems of concern to one or more constituencies whose support was essential to the long-term viability of the enterprise.

In the absence of the specific deadlines set by a legal challenge to authority, the timetable of voluntary restructuring is highly uncertain and depends on a coincidence of circumstances and events that may extend over a decade or more. At the heart of restructuring is evidence of the erosion of economic value and financial benefit associated with the strategy and structure in place. The easiest case to handle occurs when profitability is in sudden free fall and the call for action is loud and clear. However, for most large and mature corporations this is rarely the case. The evidence of deterioration is more often unclear for long periods of time and the effect is not

41

immediately life threatening. Under such circumstances, hope is sustained and organizations simply try harder to make the existing strategy work.

The imperative for change is related not simply to the immediate experience of the firm but also to the economic and social environment. If deterioration can be denied, or justified by events "beyond management's control" in the industry or the economy, it is tempting to wave off the danger signals. The environment of approval or disapproval in the actions of peers inside or outside the industry, and by those who monitor corporate performance, has much to do with individual behavior. The herd instinct is strong in business as in other human activity. The strategies and structures of the 1960s and 1970s were then as generally applauded by society as they were roundly criticized in the 1980s.

When it does occur, the sudden reversal of strategic direction is as traumatic an experience for corporate leaders as it is for their organizations. The hallmarks of leadership are a clear sense of direction, self-confidence, and persistence in the face of difficulty. The demand of leadership on the organization is unswerving loyalty to the strategy in place. Thus the buildup of inertia behind the defined corporate mission becomes intense, and a sudden and unexplained voluntary change of direction involves an inexcusable breach of the trust essential to leadership.

The successful implementation of voluntary restructuring, therefore, requires a carefully structured sequence of enabling circumstances, the timing of which is ill defined and takes patience and alertness to opportunity. Assuming that the management responsible for the strategy and structure in place is able to recognize the need for change, and willing to implement it, restructuring generally awaits the imperative of a substantial and visible deterioration of performance to signal an "external mandate" for change—the soft equivalent of a hostile attack.

If these enabling circumstances fail to materialize, the governing board and members of senior management normally defer action until the retirement of the CEO, unless the deterioration becomes imminently life threatening. The new CEO is then in a position to take his or her appointment as the mandate for change. However, given the propensity to grant the retiring CEO a strong voice in choosing his or her replacement, and to create a successor in his or her own image, the expected restructuring may not happen.

The remaining opportunity for voluntary restructuring then rests on direct intervention by a party or parties within the established governance system. There is, however, no organizational process that guarantees the existence of spontaneous agents of change within the organization at the critical juncture in corporate history. Typically, intervention relies on individuals who act on their own—who have the insight and foresight, the courage, conviction, and independence to seize the initiative.

In an economic system where response to change is largely dependent on a voluntary process, the extent and pace of voluntary restructuring appear to be, and often are, uncertain and potentially long drawn out. It is little wonder that critics of the normal corporate governance system lose their patience and turn to arbitrary intervention by self-appointed market agents of change.

Clear and Present Danger

Restructuring as a response to a hostile challenge to incumbent management is an instinctive and predictable act of self-preservation and comes as no surprise to the organization it affects. The established leadership rises to defend its prerogatives, doing whatever it takes, including, if necessary, the abandonment of long-standing strategies and structures that have been the hallmark of that prerogative.

On October 14, 1986, an investment group headed by Ronald Perelman began to acquire shares in CPC International. Through normal information channels on the Street, CPC's CEO, James Eiszner, was immediately aware that a boarding party was being prepared, and the necessity for immediate evasive action was fully apparent to him, his management, and the employees of CPC. Since 1978, Perelman had attempted a series of corporate takeover initiatives, and his hostile intentions were inescapable. Whatever the merits of the strategy and structure Eiszner had inherited from his predecessor two years earlier, it was clear that a radically different strategy and structure must be quickly implemented if he was to retain his leadership and the confidence of his investors. The details of events preceding and following this challenge from without are outlined in Chapter 8.

In a similar vein, in the fall of 1984, when Donald Clark, chief executive of Household International, rebuffed a proposal from one of his own board members, John Moran, to initiate a friendly leveraged buyout, he knew that a challenge to his authority had been joined.[1] Moran's proposal precipitated a successful defense, the ultimate outcome of which was that the carefully assembled components of the strategy and structure of the past decade would be systematically dismantled (see Chapter 4).

Real or imagined, the threat of the "barbarian at the gates" has been used for centuries by political leaders to rally their constituencies to accept radical change and sacrifice. But voluntary restructuring where no visible life-threatening event is apparent is another matter. Large organizations, like large physical objects, take enormous energy, coordination, and commitment to be set in motion in a given direction. However, once in motion they develop a powerful inertia that strongly propels them along the chosen path and is hard to deflect. Inevitably, any strategy develops a unique set of vested interests in the status quo that resists any change threatening its power, ego, and economic advantage.

Hence it is important to explore the circumstances under which incumbent management, in the absence of life-threatening circumstances, suddenly undertakes a radical new direction. What impels a change that is in direct conflict with the policy and practice the parties in power have so assiduously nurtured?

Preconditions for Voluntary Restructuring

Observation suggests that while there may be no circumstances which, singly or in combination, spontaneously induce voluntary restructuring by incumbent management, there are those which facilitate and enhance the probability that it will occur. These are the necessary, but not necessarily sufficient, conditions.

One of these is the development and dissemination of specific evidence that the strategy and structure in place is resulting in a sustained and persistent erosion of benefits flowing to one or more major corporate constituencies. In the 1970s it was the stockholder interest which perceived that this was happening to the primary indices of equity returns. Comparisons of performance against the company's own past record, against primary industry competitors, and against other industrial investments of comparable risk are all relevant. The key comparisons are not quarter to quarter or even year

---

[1] A. Fleisher, G.C. Hazard, and M.Z. Klepper, *Board Games* (Boston: Little, Brown, 1988), chap. 2, pp. 71–88.

to year, which commonly show a sawtooth progression, but over several years in which the trend line is demonstrably persistently negative. It normally takes at least five years to begin to provide proof of strategic erosion, and often a decade. Chapters 6, 7, and 8 illustrate the requisite evidence in detail.

A second precondition for potential restructuring is that this shift in the distribution of corporate value-added among primary constituencies must be accompanied by a shift in the balance of power or influence among constituencies in favor of the disadvantaged party. The concentration of voting power in the hands of investment and pension funds in the 1960s and 1970s and the availability of the capital necessary to bankroll highly leveraged takeovers placed new power in the hands of freelance agents of change prepared to take on incumbent management in the market for corporate control.

In contrast, the erosion of claims on the corporate income stream on the part of the work force, from middle management down to unionized workers through decline in job opportunity, wages, and benefits, which has characterized the early 1990s, has been accompanied by a loss of bargaining power that only full employment will restore. Only then will the investors of human capital have the potential to begin to regain some of the lost ground yielded to shareholders.

A third precondition of voluntary restructuring is the availability to incumbent management of options to bring about a substantial transformation of performance with the degree of speed and certainty sufficient to change the perceptions of, in this case, investors. One such option, for example, is the divestment of a major subsidiary that is a drag on an otherwise healthy corporate income stream. This is a particularly important precondition in that the options accessible to an outside challenger may not be available to incumbent management. Indeed, one of the key distinctions between voluntary and involuntary restructuring is that in the latter case, those who effect the change, whether incumbent management or outsiders, are able and willing to exercise options available only when circumstances appear life threatening. This contrast is discussed later in this chapter in the Safeway story.

The issue of options can be illustrated by reference to the U.S. railroad industry in the post–World War II period. A combination of circumstances in this politically sensitive industry relating to rate regulation and deregulation, industrywide labor contracts, competition from alternative passenger and freight transportation modes, and massive roadbed and equipment reinvestment needs at a time of weak financial performance deprived management of a quick fix. In response to a question concerning the possibility of a hostile takeover, Richard Bressler, CEO of the Burlington Northern railroad, would answer with a smile that his "poison pill" was the railroad itself—hard to swallow, but if swallowed, even harder to digest—and takeover agents knew it.

By contrast, other companies in other industries had a number of options for restructuring the investment portfolio and its funding that could make a material difference and, in theory at least, were equally accessible to incumbents and challengers. These are illustrated in later chapters.

A fourth precondition of restructuring, voluntary or involuntary, is leadership, the most important element, which is discussed at length in the next section.

Leadership in Place

A lot of the heat generated by investors, frustrated by what they have considered to be the leisurely pace of change in response to stockholder activism in the 1980s, has been focused on the board of directors who, presumably, are appointed to represent the stockholder interest. But fundamental change on such critically important issues as corporate strategy and structure is rarely if ever conceived and initiated by groups of people, even a group as small as a board of directors, and certainly not by collective management. In researching the form of organizational change called restructuring, we find time after time that it happens because *one* individual in a position of power "grabs the ball and runs with it."

A case in point concerns the events surrounding the restructuring of Burlington Northern, referred to above and detailed in Chapter 7. The initial strategy and structure of BN was shaped by the man who had formed it in 1970 by the merger of four railroads, Lou Menk, its first CEO and the epitome of a career railroader. Menk had begun his career as a messenger for Union Pacific at the age of nineteen, then as telegrapher for the Frisco, rising to the latter's chairman and president in 1960.

Following the OPEC energy crisis of 1973, Menk positioned BN to take advantage of the national interest in alternative energy sources, specifically coal. A large part of the nation's low-sulfur coal reserves were located in the Powder River Basin (Wyoming–Montana), uniquely served by the BN rail system. Beginning in 1975, Menk launched a six-year plan to upgrade roadbed and equipment to facilitate the exploitation of these resources. In 1980, BN reported that since 1970 the company had invested $2.7 billion, primarily to upgrade and increase rail capacity. The funding came from internal generation, including funds from the more profitable resources activities, from debt, and from the first railroad equity issue in 20 years, a convertible debenture, in 1972.

Unfortunately, there was little visible improvement in BN's financial performance. Even with the support of profits from coal, timber, and other resources, return on assets for the decade of the 1970s ranged from zero to negative in 1970 and 1971 to a high of 4% in 1979. Not surprisingly, the company's price-earnings ratio through this decade had followed a disastrously negative trend, from a high of 17 times earnings in 1970 to a low of 4 times earnings in 1979. Management continued to put a brave face on it: "Nevertheless, rail earnings have improved and we are confident they will continue to do so as we move into the 1980s."[2] However, only the most die-hard and introverted railroader could ignore the facts.

By 1977, Menk, in the midst of yet another merger, this time with the Frisco, began to shed the full responsibilities of leadership. Aged 59 in that year, he persuaded the board to appoint Norman Lorentzen, age 60, another career railroad man and trusted colleague, to the position of president and CEO while Menk remained as chairman. A man of exceptional physical and emotional energy and personal charisma, Menk had nevertheless become worn down by the burden of his office, the serious illness of his wife, and no doubt, by the apparent failure of the strategy of the 1970s to yield acceptable financial results.

It was clear that Lorentzen was an interim appointment as CEO and would not be the agent of change for the next decade. It was also clear that Menk as chairman continued to impose his vision for BN in terms which placed the railroad industry at the center of corporate strategy, and that he would prefer a like-minded successor. As the search for Lorentzen's successor got under way, one member of the board privately voiced his dissent.

This was Daniel Davisson, chief executive of the U.S. Trust Company, who had originally joined the BN board as executive vice president of Morgan Guarantee Trust. He was one in a long line of

[2] Burlington Northern, *Annual Report*, 1980.

bankers on the board who had represented the J.P. Morgan banking interests, instrumental in founding the original railroad. When Davisson joined the board, his predecessor at J.P. Morgan had alerted him to the poor financial performance and underutilization of the natural resource assets of the business. The Morgan connection undoubtedly gave Davisson a unique platform should he choose to use it, but he had to decide whether and when to exercise that choice. The board consisted primarily of Westerners representing particular regional railroad constituencies, and the few Easterners were regarded with some suspicion. He was essentially on his own.

As the search for a successor began to unfold, Davisson chose a private moment with Menk and said, in effect, "Lou, as far as I am concerned, you can have any successor you wish, as long as he is not another railroad man." To his great credit, Menk accepted the implicit criticism of his own career and set out, with the board, to find an outsider and a "generalist." The outcome of that search was the appointment of a man with whom Menk had become acquainted on the General Mills board, Richard Bressler, formerly chief financial officer and laterally executive vice president of Atlantic-Richfield Company. On his appointment as the new CEO of BN, Bressler immediately began a series of changes that radically altered the corporate and financial structure of BN, placed new emphasis on natural resources, and focused on improved financial performance. It was, in effect, a self-imposed, internally executed, financially motivated takeover.

There are many roads to Rome, but they can be taken only one road at a time, and at each turning point along the way it was one individual at BN who made the difference by exercising an option to assert leadership. Of course others were involved, and perhaps should receive credit for facilitating change. But these three people, Menk, Davisson, and Bressler, were the essential agents of change during this segment of Burlington Northern's history from 1970 to 1990.

The more one leans to the philosophy that voluntary restructuring depends on the right person in the right place at the right time, the more random and uncertain the process appears to be. However, the basic premise upon which primary dependence on voluntary restructuring is based is that, given clear evidence of persistent deterioration in overall financial performance or in the rewards to a key constituency, the pressures will sooner or later induce someone within the existing governance system to step forward to become the instrument of change. It is particularly interesting to explore what there is in common among companies that have initiated voluntary restructuring in the specific events or circumstances which triggered radical redirection.

The Triggers of Change

As I researched the specific events leading up to the decisions to implement major restructuring, it became apparent that the people involved in, or closely associated with, the decision were often reluctant to be quoted on events which touched on the character, managerial ability, or qualities of leadership of close colleagues or predecessors in office. Therefore this section will not identify the companies involved in particular examples so that the facts can be discussed more candidly.

The several factors described in this chapter as preconditions of voluntary restructuring—persuasive evidence of deterioration, empowerment of disadvantaged constituencies and their agents of change, the availability of meaningful options for positive change, and the presence of individual leadership able and willing to act—are all necessary but not fully sufficient conditions. One remains, and that is the triggering event which released the forces of change and became the rationale for a sudden departure from the status quo.

The primary obstacle to change is, of course, the predisposition of incumbent management, which "owns" the strategy and structure in place, which was its principal architect, and which built an organization around it, to persist beyond a reasonable test of effectiveness and in the face of mounting evidence of fundamental weakness. In an insightful article titled "Breach of Trust in Hostile Takeovers," Andrei Schleifer and Lawrence Summers draw attention to the complex network of formal and informal contracts that any given corporate leader creates over time in the process of building a collective commitment to a given strategy.[3] There is a high organizational cost to pay where those contracts or implicit commitments are suddenly or arbitrarily voided. No chief executive can take the resultant loss of trust lightly, since it is at the very heart of leadership and, once lost, is not easily restored.

The surprising fact is not that the present owners of a "failed" strategy do not readily confess to failure, but that some do. Of the

[3] Andrei Schleifer and Lawrence E. Summers, "Breach of Trust in Hostile Takeovers," in *Corporate Takeovers: Causes and Consequences*, Alan J. Auerbach, ed. (Chicago: University of Chicago Press, 1988), chap. 2, pp. 33–56.

nine voluntary restructurings included in this study, three were led by the same management that had been deeply associated with the previous strategy and structure. How, then, does the leadership explain to an organization, whose dedication and loyalty to the old strategy it has so carefully nurtured, the sudden reversal? Invariably it does so by using the occasion of a highly visible external event—a sudden decline in the fortunes of the company precipitated by "forces beyond its control"—to evoke the specter of mortal danger. Consider the following excerpt from an annual report:

To Our Shareholders:
    After experiencing two years of deepening recession [we] considered 1982 a critical year . . . In 1982 [we] posted [our] first yearly loss in half a century . . . We feel justified in stressing to you that those losses were not the result of a failure of your management to respond vigorously to the hard realities of our economy . . . But it was not enough because we are facing more than an unusually deep cyclical trough . . . Structural changes are taking place in the world economy . . . In order to reduce our vulnerability to an uncertain economic climate and to ensure our positions as the most efficient producer in our major markets, decisive action was required . . . These were the imperatives which led to the decisions reported to you on January 26.

    Thus, an incumbent management persuaded of the necessity for change must await a sudden and visible deterioration in fortune, which then becomes the trigger and the rationale for change—the moral equivalent of "war"—of a direct challenge to control by an outside party.
    In the absence of an incumbent management predisposed to change, or of a sudden change in the business environment or performance that offers an excuse for action, a common trigger of change is the retirement of an incumbent CEO. Restructuring is then facilitated by his or her replacement with a new CEO sufficiently distanced from the established strategy and structure that the new CEO cannot be legitimately tagged with "breach of trust." Among the three observed cases of this triggering event, one was an executive of another company, one was a former director of research in the company, and one was a former chief economist of the company. In each case, a radically new approach to strategy and structure ensued under a clear mandate for change, in which the former CEO tacitly concurred.
    However, a CEO's retirement, even at a time of serious financial

deterioration, does not guarantee a replacement with a mandate for change. One such missed opportunity is seen in the case of a CEO who had maintained a strategy about which serious doubts had developed both inside and outside the company. Eleven years into his tenure in office, and two years away from mandatory retirement, a sudden companywide decline in profitability offered the opportunity to reexamine the mature strategy. The decline, though not on its face life threatening, was a sufficient excuse for change. Not surprisingly, the soon-to-retire CEO waved off the evidence and instead endorsed as his replacement a man with similar background, experience, and priorities. Not until two years later did the new CEO, in response to a sudden takeover attempt, radically alter the course.

This leads us to the third observed trigger of voluntary restructuring, intervention by someone within the internal corporate governance structure, broadly defined, who is able to persuade or force the incumbent to a change of heart or to facilitate a change-minded replacement. Four examples were noted. One was the case of the board member previously cited in the section on leadership who, though not accelerating retirement, supported the CEO in his decision to retire early and urged an outside replacement. A second was the board member previously cited who first proposed a friendly leveraged buyout and, when that did not succeed, organized an unsuccessful hostile takeover attempt. A third was an ex-CEO and board member who initiated the early retirement of the man he had chosen to replace himself in favor of a subordinate disposed to change.

The triggering action of agents of change within the normal governance system also includes on occasion, "friendly outsiders," such as a lead bank. On one occasion, in the face of losses that threatened a loan, the lead bank worked behind the scenes to achieve the early retirement of the incumbent CEO and to accelerate his replacement with fresh leadership from within, but distanced from the prior strategy.

It is notable that there were no observable triggers of change associated with intervention by a member of the senior management team—a palace revolt. There are such occurrences, but they are rarely observable because of the strong corporate culture of loyalty and the disposition to work behind the scenes. Discussion with subordinates produced several examples in which vigorous debate and private persuasion were attempted to change the mind or timetable of an incumbent CEO, apparently without success. Yet sustained dissent must at times have an effect that is unrecognized by the outside observer.

The Voluntary Imperative

The term "voluntary imperative" for restructuring appears to be an oxymoron, since if there is an imperative for change, it is not truly voluntary. However, I have defined voluntary restructuring as one which has been accomplished within the normal governance system and without overt intervention, actual or threatened, by a hostile agent. And as we have seen, the imperatives that reside in this precondition of change, and in the events or circumstances that actually trigger it, are relative, not absolute imperatives. As stated previously, it is highly dependent on the right person in the right place at the right time under the right circumstances. At times it takes exceptional patience to await that coincidence. For some companies in the 1980s, patience ran out and confrontation occurred. Voluntary restructuring then became involuntary restructuring in which incumbent management sometimes survived, as in the three cases included in this study.

In the life history of any mature corporation, the decade-length cycle of structuring and restructuring is likely to provide examples of both voluntary and involuntary change and of the forces and counterforces that precipitate each new direction. The case history of Safeway Stores provides one such example.

It begins in 1915, when M.B. Skaggs opened a grocery store in American Falls, Idaho. Mr. Skaggs's retail food chain developed through 1926, when it merged with the Safeway chain in southern California, a merger in which Charles E. Merrill, Sr. (Merrill Lynch) had an influential role. By 1955 the company had developed substantially as an organization but was not performing well financially. In that year Merrill Lynch, one of the company's largest shareholders, pressured Safeway to replace its chief executive, and Charles Merrill, Jr., persuaded his son-in-law, Robert Magowan, to take the job.

Magowan, who had been sales manager at Merrill Lynch, could not have been better prepared to represent the self-interest of the shareholders in shaping the new strategy. He followed an aggressive path of growth both in the United States and abroad, in Canada, England, and Australia. He also improved profitability dramatically. Return on shareholders' equity (book value) rose from 8% in 1955 to 16% in 1965. The Magowan era is commonly regarded as the high point of the development of Safeway as a national and international retail food chain.

In 1969, Magowan retired as CEO but remained as chairman of

the board and subsequently chairman of the executive committee of the board through 1979. During that ten-year period, he was succeeded first by Quentin Reynolds, through 1974, then by William Mitchell. During this period Safeway surpassed A&P as the nation's largest retail food chain, but began to lose ground in financial performance.

With the benefit of hindsight, critics are unanimous that Mitchell had neither the background nor the personality essential to leadership during a decade of dynamic change in mass food distribution. With a background in controllership and lacking in hands-on retailing experience, conservative, taciturn, and cautious, Mitchell was regarded as being excessively influenced by legal and financial counsel, more concerned with defending against risk than capitalizing on opportunity. Safeway could not afford to stand still, but it did. Superstores, specialty departments, and later, scanners were transforming the marketplace. Failure to lead or keep abreast of change caused Safeway's financial performance to deteriorate. During the period 1975 to 1979, Safeway lost market share in key areas, growth in sales was cut in half, the net profit margin dropped from 1.53% to 1.04%, return on assets declined from 9.4% to 4.6%. Reflecting this trend, investors drove the price-earnings ratio down from a high of 12.3 times in 1976 to a low of 6.4 times in 1979, at a time the industry had risen to a multiple of 12. It was said that one of the principal causes was a failure to bargain aggressively with unions to hold labor costs in check.

Despite this evidence, there was no action to intervene, and Mitchell retired in 1979 at normal retirement age (65), which then became the opportunity for corporate renewal. The new chief executive was Peter Magowan, son of Robert, who at age 37 had spent the past 11 years rising through the ranks of divisional management at Safeway. The chain of shareholder representation in corporate leadership was resumed.

Recognizing the serious problems confronting the company, the younger Magowan quickly launched a major long-term voluntary restructuring, which continued year by year through 1985. The principal elements of the restructuring included

- an aggressive construction schedule of new superstores and the concurrent disposition or closing of smaller, least profitable stores and divisions. The 1982 divestiture of the Omaha division was the first major withdrawal by Safeway from a market since 1962.

- rapid expansion of new specialty departments in keeping with the trend of the times. A number of small grocery stores were converted into profitable discount Liquor Barns.
- where necessary, engaging in all-out price competition—a major departure from the past.
- a major assault on labor costs. Safeway, as the industry's most heavily unionized employer, suffered increasingly from nonunion competition.
- use of new information and control technology, including scanners.
- reduction in overhead, including nonstore management, by 15%.
- recentralization of management and the hiring of new personnel in newly created specialty areas.

The up-front costs of the intended turnaround were substantial, with the result that profit margins and return on investment declined through 1981. Then, in response to these changes and a heavy investment program, returns began to improve—slowly. The net profit margin rose from .69% in 1981 to 1.18% in 1985 and, leveraged by higher debt levels, return on equity rose from 10.3% in 1981 to 14.2% in 1983. These results were buoyed by unusual profitability overseas. The stock market responded by raising the price-earnings ratio from a multiple of 6 in 1981 to 9.6 in 1985, almost tripling the market value of the stock. By normal standards this would be regarded as a highly successful restructuring. Analysts were generally supportive of Magowan's leadership, but some worried about the *pace* of change.

They, and Magowan, had reason to worry. Food retailers generally, and Safeway in particular, were a tempting target for takeover specialists, owing to their

- large and highly stable cash flows, well suited to the servicing of debt;
- readily divisible and marketable assets, which could be segmented and sold to generate quick cash;
- extensive real estate investments booked at below-market values;
- cost structures vulnerable to hard-nosed renegotiation and "downsizing."

Takeover rumors had stimulated the price of Safeway stock during 1985. On June 13, 1986, the Dart Group announced that it had acquired 5.9% of Safeway stock. Safeway was then "in play," and to Magowan's deep disappointment, the restructuring process was no longer voluntary. The stock, which had been selling around $40, was up for bid by the Haft family at $58 cash. Buying time with legal skirmishing, Safeway considered a number of alternatives to save its independence, but none offered any lasting protection. Finally, on July 28, Safeway announced an agreement with Kohlberg, Kravis and Roberts to take the company private in a highly leveraged buyout. Magowan would remain as CEO.

In the two years that followed the privatization of Safeway, a sharply accelerated restructuring occurred which made the actions taken in the previous six years pale by comparison.

- Sales declined from $20 billion to $14 billion and employees from 185,000 to 106,000;
- 1,100 stores were sold, including the highly profitable U.K. operation;
- corporate staff was reduced from 1,200 to 670;
- capital spending was cut in half;
- operating costs, including particularly labor costs, were sharply reduced.

The net result was, for the time being at least, a much smaller, more focused, more efficient, and more profitable Safeway.

In commenting on these events, and the contrast between voluntary and involuntary restructuring, Peter Magowan has said:

The first question most usually asked when I tell this story is: Why couldn't you or why didn't you do all those things when you were still a public company? My answer is to basically agree with the criticism that we could have done more than we did, but *we could not have done what we did do without going through the incredible trauma and pressure of the LBO.*

First, could we have done more? I think it's important to recognize that our asset sales and expense reduction effort did not start when we did the LBO. We sold our operations in Toronto, Australia, Memphis, Butte, Pennsylvania all in the '82–'85 time frame. As for cost control, we reduced distribution expense every year from 1979 to 1985. Our U.S. non-store headcount was reduced by 22% from the end of 1979 to the end of 1985. We consolidated our U.S. divisions from 21 in 1979 to 15 in 1985; in fact, it was these improvements in ridding ourselves of underperforming stores and reducing expense that allowed us to more than double our earnings from 1981 to 1985—from $108 million to $231 million.

So, could we have done still more? Yes, in retrospect—and it is a lot easier to answer this question with the benefit of hindsight—we could have done more. But I don't think we could ever have done what we did without going through the LBO. Let's look at expense reduction. It's not easy to get your people to cut all the unnecessary expense they can when you are producing record profit. It is not easy to get the labor concessions you deserve when the unions read your annual report and its references to "record profit." We asked the unions to give us the concessions before the buyout. They were either unwilling or unable to do so. But once the buyout occurred it was possible to create a total transformation of corporate culture.[4]

The Safeway experience points up very clearly the contrast between voluntary and involuntary restructuring—in this case under the same chief executive. The difference is less *in the nature* of the changes designed to restore a higher return on investment but rather primarily *in the pace or time frame* of change and *in the degree* of change. Large organizations rarely initiate drastic and rapid redirection without a visible threat to the solvency or independence of the enterprise or its incumbent management. To expand on Magowan's statement, it was the imminent loss of control to the Dart Group, the sudden concentration of power in the hands of KKR, with its renowned hard-headed focus on ownership value, and in particular, the relentless discipline of servicing a huge debt burden that created the "incredible trauma" and suddenly accelerated the pace of change.

Magowan also explains the difficulty of forcing major restructuring in the absence of imminent danger. Every company is, at any given moment, in the process of implementing a strategy designed to improve performance and of enlisting the full support of the entire corporate community in this effort. For a company committed to one strategic direction, it is difficult then to plan and initiate another and conflicting strategy simultaneously. This is particularly difficult if the strategy in place continues to be led by those who conceived and initiated it, if the strategy shows signs of success, and if the investment community manifests a positive response.

---

[4]Peter A. Magowan, address to the Stanford Business School Alumni Association, October 11, 1988.

CHAPTER 4

Changing the Structure
of Corporate Investment

Chapter Overview

Most of the attention directed to financial restructuring in the 1980s has been focused on the effect on the market value of owners' equity. The most dramatic examples of the benefits of restructuring record the sudden surge in market expectations when a contest for control and the prospect for a change in management leads to a bidding war for the stock and rapid escalation of the price. These stock market expectations anticipate that, either as a result of new ownership or defensive response, there will be fundamental changes in the financial management of the corporation resulting in higher return on investment (ROI).

This study focuses not on shareholder expectations, but on corporate performance—on the factors that lead to improvement in ROI and, more particularly, in return on the shareholders' equity investment. Stated in its simplest terms, ROI can be improved in one or both of two ways: increasing the return or reducing the investment. Chapter 4 examines the nature of fundamental changes in the structure of corporate investment leading to economies in the use of equity dollars. Chapter 5 examines the nature of fundamental changes in structure of the corporate revenue stream leading to increased residual returns to the owners. Working together, these changes often produced substantial improvement in the level of return on equity, which, in turn, justified rising expectations in the stock markets.

One way to characterize the change in the corporate environment of the late 1970s and the 1980s is to describe it as a breakdown of investor confidence in the ability or willingness of professional managers as responsive custodians of the owners' investment. Those of us who experienced the post–World War II period as adults can remember a time when professional business management in America was heralded as a model of efficient organizational leadership. Over time there was an increasing suspicion that the natural instincts of career professionals led them to place the well-being of long-term investors of human capital, including themselves, ahead of the well-being of investors of financial capital.

The erosion of trust between a principal (the owner) and his or her agent (the manager) produces a natural desire to limit the agent's discretion over the investment of corporate funds. The restructuring of the 1980s reduced management discretion over investment in four important ways:

1. By reducing the flow of unrestricted funds provided by the automatic reinvestment of retained earnings. Restructuring forced many companies to disgorge more of the annual operating cash flow through higher levels of dividend payout and stock repurchases, thus returning these funds to the discretion of investors.

2. By renouncing the strategy of product-market diversification and refocusing investment on the core business. It was a return to an emphasis on quality over quantity, on profitability per unit of investment over aggregate earnings. In the process, a number of business segments that had been shown to lack critical mass and clear long-term competitive advantage were dumped overboard. This distinctive feature of the 1980s was a clear rejection of the notion that the individual industrial corporation could be an effective vehicle of portfolio diversification for its shareholders.

3. By a decline in the proportion of invested capital allowed to remain for long periods of time in passive or liquid form (reserves) at low rates of return under the unrestricted authority of management as to whether, when, and where to recommit it to active use. Liquidity can be apparent in asset form—cash equivalents or other redundant assets—or in underutilized debt

capacity. Both grew in the 1970s and, where most evident, were an open invitation for raiders to fund a takeover with the company's own assets.

4. By a major shift in the form and conditions of corporate funding, reducing significantly the proportion of funding from equity claims with minimal investor control over purpose or conditions of use, repayment, compensation, or penalty for non-compliance, and substituting debt contracts, which in all these dimensions are more defined and restrictive. A sharp increase in the debt-equity ratio was most rapidly accomplished by a simultaneous increase in debt to fund a repurchase of equity.

Taken together, these changes could and did make a material difference to the size of the equity base and therefore to the return on equity (ROE). They were, however, not without cost to the firm or to the constituencies other than the shareholder. A leaner corporate balance sheet means that the shock of unexpected events is transmitted more rapidly and directly to those involved in day-to-day operations. A quicker response is required to protect continuity and solvency. Higher returns to equity holders come at a price of increased risk in financial and operating ratios, which impose greater volatility in earnings and cash flows. Finally, organizational and financial slack in these various forms is a persistent characteristic of human enterprise. The discipline required for a high degree of financial efficiency is difficult to sustain, and the improved ROEs of the 1980s may have misled investors into unrealistic expectations for the longer term.

Restricting the Authority to Reinvest

During the 1960s and 1970s, the preference of corporate managements to emphasize financial self-sufficiency and to reduce reliance on the capital markets meant that most new investment by established corporations was free of any need for prior clearance or approval by investors or their financial intermediaries. Internally generated funds plus conservative increments of debt were generally sufficient to fund the entire corporate strategy. With the de-emphasis of dividends in the package of equity holder rewards, and the maintenance of moderate debt levels, only a modest fraction of the net funds generated by product-market investment were returned to either equity or debt holders for external reinvestment. Hence the investment base of many corporations was steadily expanding.

The restructuring of the 1980s challenged the automatic reinvestment of internally generated funds and caused many corporations to return larger amounts of capital to the capital markets, principally to equity holders in the form of increased dividends and stock repurchase. This would be readily anticipated in the case of companies that had committed gross errors of judgment in investment and, therefore, where management was no longer trusted. It is less obvious why this would apply to well-managed and relatively profitable businesses. Yet there was clearly a general shift going on in management's perception of discretionary authority.

This general change in attitude is best illustrated by the case of General Mills, a company with a long-standing reputation inside and outside its industry for profitability and superior management. During the 1960s and 1970s, General Mills followed a strategy of aggressive diversification, which diminished its dependence on its traditional markets in flour and packaged convenience foods. This produced a new growth momentum and improving profitability. Throughout the 1970s the company steadily improved overall return on equity (at book value) from 16% to 19%. However, the new corporate leadership installed in 1981 recognized that the mood of the capital markets had changed. Diversification of corporate product markets was no longer in vogue and appeared to have a negative impact on price-earnings ratios. A general mistrust of the priorities of corporate management was gaining popular acceptance among equity investors. The management of General Mills began to take actions to restore investor confidence.

One action concerned the distribution of funds flows. Figure 4.1 presents an overview of the pattern of the flow of funds for General Mills for a 20-year period, from 1968 to 1989. The data represent my reconstruction of General Mills' net flow of funds to and from the product and capital markets. The primary flows from the product markets were net flows from operations, adjusted for changes in working capital. The primary flows to the capital markets were dividends, repurchase of stock, interest, and repayment of debt, offset on occasion by new infusions of debt and equity. The net product-market flows over the two decades are entirely positive and growing, with the occasional decline—notably, in 1985, when major restructuring was implemented. The net capital-market flows, which were predominantly negative (outflows), accelerated in the 1980s.

During the period 1970 to 1979 inclusive, the total net outflow of funds from General Mills to the capital markets was $358 million,

Figure 4.1 General Mills Flow of Funds

or 25% of the total net inflow from the product markets. During the period 1980 to 1989 inclusive, the total net outflow to the capital markets was $2.163 billion, or 59% of the total net inflow from the product markets. Thus, even in one of the companies most trusted by investors, there was a major decline in the proportion of internally generated funds automatically reinvested in the company operations.

Although this was an entirely voluntary decision by an incumbent management, it reflected the changing mood of the investment community and its desire to see a higher proportion of corporate earnings recycled through the capital markets before reinvestment was confirmed.

Limiting Investment Choice

Perhaps the most fundamental change brought about by the restructuring of the 1980s was the reversal of the trend to diversification of corporate revenue streams that occurred in the heyday of organizational growth. In identifying and refocusing on core competence, businesses shed underperforming divisions and subsidiaries and, at least temporarily, shrank the investment base substantially.

The history of Household Finance Corporation (HFC), founded in 1878 by Frank Mackey in Minneapolis to make consumer loans available to individuals of modest means, provides a dramatic illustration of the life cycle of corporate diversification. For the first 80 years of its history, the company grew to provide a national network of loan offices targeted at a mass consumer market. In 1961, H.E. MacDonald, a CEO who had come to HFC from Montgomery Ward, began a new era of wide-ranging diversification with the acquisition of the Coast-to-Coast hardware chain. His goal was to offset the inherent cyclicality of consumer lending, to provide an investment vehicle for the large cash flow generated by consumer lending, and to move into lines of business with which he was personally familiar.

By 1971, when MacDonald retired, HFC had expanded the merchandising business into variety stores, grocery stores, and home furnishings. It had also entered manufacturing through the acquisition of King-Seeley Thermos Co. and leasing through the acquisition of National Car Rental. Thus by 1971, HFC, which had become Household International, was a true conglomerate, a term for which even current management makes no apologies.

A decade later, Household International had reached the highwater mark of unrelated diversification. With over $7 billion of gross revenues, 41% of 1981 income came from nine separate entities in diversified financial services, 29% from 10 merchandising enterprises, 18% from 20 manufacturing businesses, and 11% from 4 transportation service activities. Businesses ranged from banking and insurance to supermarkets, plumbing fixtures, car rental, and an airline.

In November 1982, Gilbert Ellis, CEO since 1973, died suddenly, and Donald Clark was appointed chief executive officer to succeed him. In his first statement to shareholders, in February 1983, Clark announced that "with Household's major diversification goals completed, we are in the process of assimilating and realigning the components . . . [involving] a careful review of each business." As is true of most voluntary restructuring, the refocusing process was at first imperceptible, involving small changes at the fringe of corporate activity. With Household, it resulted in the sale of Wien Air Alaska (1983) and the furniture operations (1984).

Household management was well aware that conglomerates were a particular target of the rising tide of hostile takeover activity. There was growing acceptance in the investment community of the idea that the market applied a discount to conglomerate equities owing to the arbitrary bundling of businesses of unequal return. The specific event that triggered an acceleration of Household's restructuring came from an unusual direction—namely, within its own boardroom. One of Household's board members was John Moran of the investment firm of Dyson-Kissner-Moran. In 1984 this firm owned 6.8% of Household's stock. Moran first proposed to include management in a friendly leveraged buyout involving the sale of the financial services division as a key source of funding. When this offer was rebuffed and Household adopted its shareholder rights plan in August 1984, Moran initiated litigation challenging that plan.

The ensuing legal battle over the validity of Household's takeover defenses, a story in itself, was fought through to the Delaware Supreme Court. In November 1985, the court, in a landmark decision, upheld Household's "poison pill" defense. In the meantime, however, Household had begun to explore divestment of the entire merchandising operation. It was first offered to the Jewel Companies, a diversified retail chain, in June 1984, but no agreement was reached. In October 1985, a deal was struck in which an outside group of investors, together with some of the merchandising unit's management, paid $825 million ($700 million cash) for 90% of the equity of a new independent merchandising company. In January 1986, the board voted to use the proceeds to repurchase up to 22% of the company's outstanding shares. During 1986, Household repurchased at market price 25% of its outstanding common stock, and equivalents, including the holdings of the Moran group, thereby ending any takeover interest.

Subsequently Household continued to restructure while continuing to diversify and expand financial services and manufacturing. The restructuring included the discontinuance of certain industrial products and the sale, in 1986, of National Car Rental. Through 1988, Household continued to acquire new manufacturing businesses. On January 11, 1989, Household announced the divestiture of its entire manufacturing operation through the spin-off of three independent manufacturing companies: Eljer (building products), Schwitzer (engine components), and Scotsman (refrigeration), and the sale of the remainder.

With this action, Household had closed a 30-year chapter of unrelated diversification to refocus exclusively on the market sector where it began—financial services. It was, however, a radically transformed and diversified financial services company: consumer banking, credit cards, mortgages, commercial and retail credit, and insurance. The entire process of disengagement from unrelated diversification and return to a single product-market focus had taken Clark 7 years to implement.

In a comment on the recent restructuring included in the 1988 annual report, Household's management said:

The company sold its Transportation business in 1986 and its Merchandising business in 1985. On January 11, 1989, the company announced a plan to distribute to its common shareholders new shares, to be publicly traded, in three manufacturing companies. The companies will be created from units which, at December 31, 1988, comprised the major part of the company's Manufacturing business . . . The company believes its Financial Services and Manufacturing businesses have very different operating, financial and investment characteristics. Separating these businesses into discrete companies will allow each business to pursue its own mission more vigorously, achieve appropriate market recognition of its performance and produce administrative savings. Management believes that shares of the new manufacturing companies will trade at higher market valuations than these businesses have been accorded as part of Household International.

The restructuring met with apparent shareholder approval (see Figure 4.2). The close-up figures show the market responses on the days the three major divestments were announced. In all three cases there was a significant positive, market-adjusted response ranging from 1.7% for the merchandising divestment to 8.6% for the manufacturing divestment. (Market-adjusted returns are the change in value of Household stock in excess of the market change as measured by the S&P 500.) Clearly, the market approved.

Contracting Discretionary Reserves

The consequences of the manifest erosion of trust in professional corporate management on the part of investors in the 1980s were reflected not only in a reduction in the proportion of operating inflows available to management for automatic reinvestment and in the range of investment options but also in the proportion of invested capital residing for extended periods of time in passive or discretionary reserves. These reserves exist not only in surplus cash or cash-equivalent investments but also in unused investment-grade debt capacity. The corporate risk-relieving function of such ready reserves when compared with the opportunity cost to investors was no longer considered a sufficient reason to tolerate the high levels of liquidity found in many companies in the 1960s and 1970s.

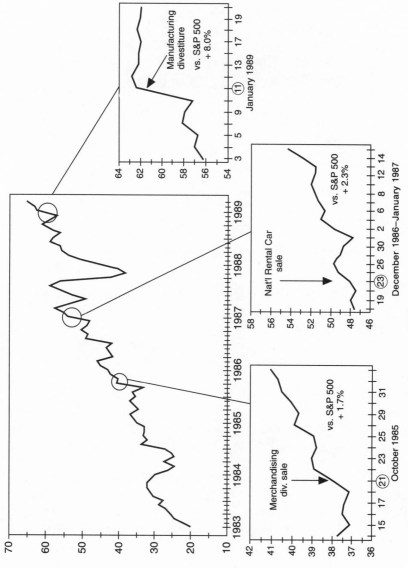

Figure 4.2 Household International Stock Price

Source: Standard & Poor's COMPUSTAT.

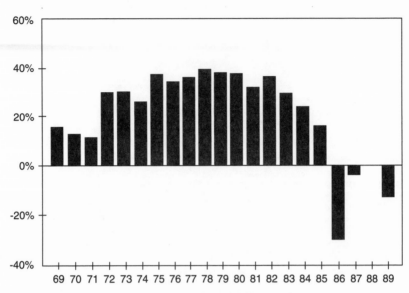

Figure 4.3   CPC International Liquidity Index

Source: Standard & Poor's COMPUSTAT.

As a measure of this liquidity, I have constructed a liquidity index that shows cash reserves plus unused debt capacity as a percentage of shareholders' equity at book value.[1] Figure 4.3 shows the liquidity index for CPC International for the period 1969 to 1989.

CPC International is a major international food products company.[2] The figure shows the steady buildup of liquidity through the 1970s. This buildup ended in 1983, when the CEO, James McKee, announced a major capital-expenditure program, called Investment for Growth, designed to improve the competitive edge in both major product lines: corn wet-milling and branded grocery products. In the fall of 1986, a hostile takeover bid launched by Ronald Perelman triggered a vigorous and ultimately successful defense.

In the process, however, not only were all of CPC's customary liquid reserves consumed, but they went sharply negative, judged by historical standards. It is assumed that had Perelman been successful

[1] Unused (long-term) debt capacity is derived by comparing current debt levels with the maximum debt-equity ratio previously approved by company management for normal corporate borrowing purposes.

[2] See Chapter 8 for the complete story of the CPC restructuring.

he would likewise have dried up corporate liquidity in funding the takeover. In either case, it left management without its accustomed contingency reserve and, therefore, on a much tighter rein from the investment community. The contingency reserve had provided management with a critical defensive resource when under attack, though it is impossible to say whether such a contingency had motivated its accumulation.

For some companies, what I have referred to here as the liquidity index is only part of the broader liquidity strategy and structure. There are two other components. One is the discretionary reserve built into the investment in working capital. This is impossible for an outside observer to quantify accurately, but operating management knows where it exists and the process by which it can be released. The widespread popularity in the United States in the 1980s of the Japanese-style "just-in-time inventories" was part of the squeeze on discretionary reserves.

The other major component of corporate liquidity strategy and structure is the segmentation of product-market investment discussed in the previous section. The wave of product-market diversification peculiar to the 1960s and 1970s can be characterized as a long-term liquidity strategy in which large sums of internally and externally generated funds were "parked" in active and desired profitable investment, to be later liquidated in efficiently separable segments, at a time unspecified, to defend and reinvigorate the core of the corporate enterprise. This dimension of long-term liquidity was more apparent in the case of Household International than in that of CPC. CPC's industrial products division (corn wet-milling) was more of an integrated operation and hence more difficult to liquidate sequentially than was its packaged grocery products division. Nevertheless the antitakeover defense demonstrated the critical role of rapid unbundling of segmented investment in preserving corporate independence.

Tightening the Terms of Funding

The fourth major change in the structure of corporate investment that reduced management discretion was in the terms and conditions of the funding of investment, primarily because of a major shift in the mix of debt and equity in the long-term capital structure of the firm.

The contractual form of long-term funding, which offers management maximum discretion, is obviously common equity: no repayment, no mandatory compensation for use, automatic reinvestment of earnings, no covenants restricting or defining how the funds are to be used. What best serves "the stockholder interest" is left for management to define. Debt contracts, on the other hand, provide funds for a limited period of time, require regular compensation for use, and often restrict both the use to which the funds are put and the conditions under which continued employment is permitted.

There has been a general predisposition in the post–Great Depression era to approve of "conservative" financial policy, which sharply limits the magnitude of debt leverage, thus reducing the risk of default—i.e., the risk of triggering investor intervention in the financial management process. An A bond rating was a very good thing; a triple-A bond rating was best of all.

There is, however, another side to the leverage issue. It has to do with investor trust in the competence and loyalty of professional managers—loyalty to stockholder priorities. A decline in trust on the part of the capital markets would suggest a shift in the balance of funding contracts away from the least restrictive (common equities) toward the more restrictive (debt or debt-equity hybrids). It ensures that more of the flow of funds will be regularly recycled through the capital markets, requiring regular reapproval and possible redefinition of purpose and conditions of use. Instances of both voluntary and involuntary restructuring in the 1980s commonly involved substantial releveraging through both increased debt and, more significant, shrinkage of the equity base through stock repurchase. The motivation of management that cooperated in these changes was often self-preservation, but the price to be paid was reduced control over the flow of funds.

To illustrate this aspect of restructuring, I refer again to the history of CPC. Figure 4.4 shows the debt-equity ratio for CPC from 1972 to 1987. The proportion of debt in the long-term capital structure declined steadily from 1972 to 1980, rose in 1981, and declined to the 1980 level in 1982. Then, from 1982 to 1986, the ratio rose sharply, driven by two forces. One was a major long-term capital investment program. The second, and more important, was a major stock repurchase program triggered by a hostile takeover attempt. As a result, the debt-equity ratio rose from 18% in 1982 to 86% in 1986. Outstanding long-term debt rose from $193 million in 1982 to $806 million in 1986, and shareholders' equity declined from $1.305 billion in 1982 to $956 million in 1986. Clearly, the discipline imposed by

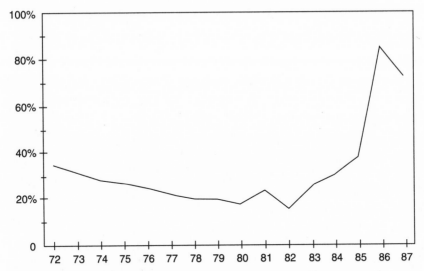

Figure 4.4   CPC International Debt-to-Equity Ratio

Source: Standard & Poor's COMPUSTAT.

annual debt servicing, maturity dates, and restrictive covenants was much more pronounced than in the 1970s. That the pressure of this discipline was sharply felt is evident in the rapidity with which highly leveraged restructuring strategies were returned to normal debt levels as opportunity permitted. The mandate of high-leverage repayment schedules imposed harsh cash flow and investment controls on the affected companies during the post-restructuring period. However, the haste to scale down debt and the success of that program raise a question as to how lasting the new investment discipline will be when debt returns to normal once the danger is past.

Enhancing the Productivity of Dollars Invested

Each of the four dimensions of balance sheet restructuring described in the preceding sections has the intent of ensuring that every equity dollar invested is actively employed in generating the greatest return to the shareholder. When employed collectively, as they were to some degree in all three of the companies used to illustrate each aspect, the productive power of a given investment of equity capital can be greatly enhanced:

- A smaller fraction of equity capital is employed per dollar of corporate investment.
- A smaller fraction of corporate investment is employed in non-productive (passive) uses.
- A smaller fraction of active product-market corporate investment is employed outside the primary and most profitable area of activity.
- A smaller fraction of the funds produced by this corporate investment is automatically reinvested without capital-market review.

The net result is a much leaner balance sheet. From the equity investor viewpoint, it means a more efficient allocation of invested capital and a higher ROI.

It is important to note that each of these changes can be implemented simply by executive order, with the approval of the board: changing the dividend payout, repurchasing blocks of common stock, shutting down or disposing of operating businesses or other corporate assets, raising the level of debt financing. At the core of the "quick fix" of corporate restructuring of the 1980s, they were the favored tools of both aggressive and defensive strategies to bring a sudden surge of new value to the equity market. This is in marked contrast to the second component of improvement in ROI, the restructuring of the revenue stream, or the income statement, which often involves long-drawn-out renegotiation of contracts with various corporate constituencies, a process much better suited to the experience and talents of professional managers than to capital-market agents of change, or even to an aroused board of directors. These differences in approach and timing of restructuring options are described in the next chapter.

CHAPTER 5

Changing the Structure
of the Revenue Stream

Chapter Overview

The restructuring of a balance sheet, the objective of which is to produce a leaner and more focused base of investment, must be accompanied by a restructuring of the income statement. References to the balance sheet and the income statement are used as shorthand descriptors for the sets of issues related to the base of invested capital on the one hand, and the flow of funds derived from investment on the other. The flow of funds includes, of course, both the cost and revenue structure. Owing to inherent rigidities in this cost and revenue structure, a shrinking investment base could adversely affect return on investment unless these rigidities were aggressively attacked. Any comprehensive plan to improve corporate ROI includes a critical examination of all elements of cost.

A "meat ax" approach to cost cutting can produce sudden and dramatic improvement in profitability, and in an emergency the instinctive response of management is to mandate an across-the-board cut in all expenditures. However, our primary interest in successful long-term financial restructuring is in economies that can be sustained in the long term. Periods of sustained profitability and growth are inevitably accompanied by slack in the system and creeping inefficiencies, which are confronted only in times of financial stress. The goal of restructuring the revenue stream is to create a new climate of cost containment and revenue enhancement, in the process of which structural rigidities can be reduced or eliminated.

This chapter begins with the story of Armco, which in 1982 was confronted with the sudden collapse of profitability and the immediate necessity of drastic restructuring of investment and revenues in order simply to survive. Such emergencies can produce an openness and candor that allows an outside observer an unusual glimpse into real-world priorities at work. It shows the integration of investment and revenue restructuring, first to generate cash flows essential to survival, second to restore profitability, and finally to provide a firm base upon which subsequent growth and profitability can be sustained.

We then turn to cases that illustrate the potential for restructuring of the two principal components of the income stream: corporate overhead and the cost of operations. The restructuring of corporate overhead is illustrated in the downsizing of Safeway's headquarters operations following the leveraged buyout by Kohlberg, Kravis and Roberts. This is admittedly an extreme example, but as such, it illustrates in unmistakable detail the cost elements that comprise the overlay of corporate management and oversight.

The most fundamental and important element of cost restructuring concerns the distribution of the claims on the corporate revenue stream by the primary contributors to the productive process. Over time, a series of contractual agreements designed to stabilize costs in a growing market become obstacles when the market and the competitive environment undergo radical change. A redistribution of claims on the future revenue stream is essential if the residual return to shareholders is to be enhanced. This is the most difficult, and important, of all structural changes to achieve. We discover what happens when a new owner renegotiates these contracts for a failing subsidiary of a mining company.

Finally, we bring together the combined effects of one company's financial restructuring to observe the impact of changes in profit margin, investment, and funding on the long-term return on equity and the response of the investment community to the changing trends in financial performance. The company in question is Household International, whose investment portfolio restructuring was described in Chapter 4. The resultant impact on investment, funding, and revenue stream are demonstrated in the long-term movements of return on investment and return on equity, the bottom line of corporate performance. We also observe the response of investors to evidence of fundamental, sustained improvement in their claim on the wealth created by corporate enterprise.

Armco's Survival Plan

In Chapter 2, I described the evolution of Armco's financial strategy and structure in the 1960s and 1970s. As a leading U.S. steel manufacturer, Armco experienced the severe stresses placed on that industry by the rebuilding of European and Japanese steel capacity after World War II and the changes in technology which introduced new domestic competition for integrated steel companies. Its response, typical of American industry in the postwar period, was to diversify into related and unrelated industries. That strategy came suddenly into question in 1982 when, as a result of the concurrent collapse of its major product markets in steel and oil field equipment and supplies, and overexpansion and overexposure in insurance coverage, 54 years of unbroken profitability suddenly turned into a $345 million loss. It was a bitter pill for the CEO, Harry Holliday, who, in 1981, as the first major step to mark his incumbency, had announced "a new dawn for steel" and a $700 million plan to increase steel capacity.

Needless to say, the new dawn was quickly placed on hold and, under severe cash flow pressures, expansion plans were replaced by a "survival plan." Nervous investors watched as Armco's bond ratings were lowered. A major component of structural downsizing was apparent in the Armco payroll. In 1982, as part of a broad reduction in employment, Armco initiated an early retirement plan, for which special charges amounted to $30 million that year. The targeted savings from payroll reduction were $100 million a year.

The pressure to cut back the scale of operations to generate cash flow and restore profitability continued through 1983 and 1984, which were also loss years. The track record with respect to employment costs is seen in the following numbers:

	1981	1982	1983	1984
Total employees	67,660	52,013	48,071	44,383
Wages & salaries (millions)	$1,354	$1,270	$1,075	$1,045
Benefits (millions)	$ 614	$ 641	$ 568	$ 551
Total costs per employee (thousands)	$ 29	$ 37	$ 34	$ 36

Substantial cuts were achieved, but it is apparent that by 1984 there was rising resistance to further reductions in the scale of operations, and costs per employee were beginning to increase again.

By the summer of 1984, the cash flow crisis at Armco had become intense. In August, Armco had its annual strategy meeting. Despite the immediate financial crisis, the long-term strategy was still driven by an expansion mentality. President and COO Robert Boni chose that meeting to confront the issue by arguing for a general sell-off of its operating units, and tried to convince Holliday and the top management team. He put a list of units for sale on the blackboard. Not surprisingly, there were no volunteers among the group VPs to put their units on the auction block. The units were removed from the board one by one. The plan failed to gain the commitment of Holliday, who stated, "There will be a morale problem if we do this."

In October 1984, Holliday suffered a heart attack and Boni became the new CEO. He immediately swung into a full-speed restructuring, which he called A Strategy of Transition. In a remarkably frank and detailed statement of the plan, made public in the annual report of 1985, Boni presented the bitter medicine. Some excerpts follow.

Armco's recovery will follow a two-part strategic path. The initial phase, which began in 1985 and will continue through 1986, concentrates on restoring the financial health and stability of Armco by cutting costs, conserving cash, improving profitability and finding ways to reduce our debt and eliminate the burden of high interest expense. The second phase will concentrate on growth—built around profitable core operations.

This discussion of the events and accomplishments of 1985 concentrates on the "corporate" aspects of Armco.

The First Quarter: A Strategy for Survival

The beginning of 1985 saw Armco in a precarious position. The company had sustained losses totaling $1.3 billion since 1981. We were saddled with a heavy debt and interest burden. We were negotiating for extension of waivers of bank covenants because of non-compliance and were unable to borrow under our revolving credit agreement. Shareholders' equity had fallen below $1 billion for the first time in years. Uncertainties in the insurance industry, and in the demands state insurance regulators could make upon our struggling insurance companies, threatened the very existence of Armco.

We already had taken many painful steps to stabilize our financial health. Plants had been shut down, the entire work force greatly reduced, and large reductions made in working capital—all in an effort to make our continuing operations profitable and generate cash to reduce our mountainous debt.

Unfortunately, these steps still were not enough. For example, despite an earlier infusion of capital into our insurance operations, three state insurance commissioners questioned whether our domestic companies in run-off[1] had sufficient assets to cover possible future claims. Had any one of those commissioners taken action against any of our insurance companies before we could develop a successful plan to strengthen the companies, our lenders could have demanded accelerated payment of approximately $600 million of our debt and guarantees.

Clearly, our efforts had to be concentrated on the short term: the day-to-day survival of Armco. And so, as the quarter unfolded, we outlined six objectives we felt had to be accomplished to ensure the survival of our company:

1. Develop a plan to enhance our insurance capital
2. Negotiate new bank agreements
3. Develop a divestment program that would generate cash and move the company out of markets with limited potential for Armco
4. Establish an overall debt reduction program
5. Further reduce costs and overheads as quickly and responsibly as possible
6. Develop an overall corporate strategy that would work to strengthen our balance sheet and provide a foundation for the future.

Here's how those objectives were met.

The report went on to detail actions taken to shore up the reserves of the insurance operation and to renegotiate loan agreements with banks. It then continued:

Establishment of a Cash Generation Plan

Simultaneously, we developed a two-pronged cash generation plan. Obviously, one way to generate cash is to conserve cash, and that meant

---

[1] The term "run-off" refers to an operation in which no new policies are sold but existing policies must be maintained and claims honored.

significant reductions in operating expenses—including employment. Our selling and administrative expenses represented 9% of sales for the year 1984. We wanted to reduce it further by the end of 1985.

The second part of the cash generation plan involved selling assets.

The focus on cash generation was the key to near-term survival, just as a return to sustained profitability was the key to long-term survival. In 1985, Boni could not have known how long it would take to complete the downsizing and restructuring process, which in fact continues into the early 1990s by further concentration on the specialty steel business. By 1987, employment had been cut by more than 50%, with the highly troubling prospect that the company had as many workers on retirement compensation as it had on its active work force. Disengagement from the ill-advised foray into insurance proved to be a tar baby of near disastrous proportions. Between 1984 and 1991, the company was forced to infuse new cash into the run-off insurance operations to the amount of $600 million, and large write-offs of prior investment persistently eroded profitability and equity as late as 1991.

The burden imposed on a company half its former size by commitments assumed in the heyday of expansion illustrates the sustained drag on the restructuring and recovery process from the mistakes of the past and why so many companies have chosen bankruptcy and default as the way out. Though Armco had no choice but to honor its obligations to insurance policyholders, it nevertheless took the honorable and painful path to restoration of its financial integrity. The return to a highly focused and profitable specialty steel company was a long road, which Boni was unable to see through to the end. He retired as CEO in 1990 and was succeeded by his second in command, Robert Purdum.

The Corporate Superstructure

A natural target for structural improvement in the revenue stream is the layer of expense associated with corporate management, information, and services. Inevitably, periods of sustained profitability and capital abundance lead to slack in the system. At best there is a tenuous connection between some areas of corporate expenditure and current revenue and, where there is a connection, the marginal return may not stand up to an objective test.

One of the inevitable consequences of corporate growth in size and diversity in an era of professionalization of management was a rising cost of administrative information, control, and oversight. New layers of middle management and new staff functions were justified on the grounds that they increased the ability of top management to monitor and direct an increasingly complex—and remote—productive operation. The change was gradual, and the financial burden of a payroll with an ill-defined relationship to value-added was acceptable as long as profits and cash flows were in a positive trend. New, campuslike corporate headquarters were the most visible symbol of organizational slack.

An example of aggressive shrinkage of the headquarters managerial structure is that of the leveraged buyout and privatization of Safeway beginning in November 1986 (see Chapter 3). When Peter Magowan became chief executive in 1979, he began a major effort to renew the competitive performance of Safeway and to improve its efficiency and profitability. The program of voluntary restructuring, previously cited, included a 33% reduction in nonstore head count between 1980 and 1986. In contrast to later reductions, the voluntary downsizing proceeded at a slower pace, relying on the less painful process of natural attrition. Of the later—involuntary—period, Magowan has said: "The discipline of [inflated] debt forced better capital spending decisions . . . It is just easier to be lean and mean when you are private. It is tough to get management to cut out people when you are reporting 'record profits.' When you are reporting record debt it is amazing what you can do without."

The impact of the LBO on headquarters expenses is seen in the following figures. (It should be noted that Safeway's headquarters were anything but luxurious to begin with. They have been and continue to be located in an old warehouse building in a low-rent district of Oakland, California.)

Safeway Corporate Headquarters Expense

	Dollars (thousands)	Head Count
1985	$62,784	1,219
1986	55,379	908
1987	46,917	745
1988	42,468	634

The layoffs resulting from the LBO occurred in two stages, the first a mandated 30% cut across the board and the second more selective, correcting some excesses. Examples of the cuts:

1. facilities engineering, reduced from 150 to 5 employees
2. advertising, reduced from 20 to 3 employees
3. elimination of a word-processing department (300)
4. elimination of one computer center (from 2)
5. printing operations eliminated
6. corporate jet sold

Of course, layoffs cost money too, including, in this case, the out-of-court settlement of a wrongful termination class-action suit for $8.2 million. Unfortunately, many of the people fired in haste were very good employees, as Magowan himself concedes, and the pain of sudden termination was extensive. In part, the cutbacks involved the substitution of outsourcing for products and services previously produced in-house. The figures cited above show a 48% reduction in head count, corresponding to only a 32% reduction in dollars expended.

These drastic reductions in corporate overhead show in sharp detail the potential for the realignment of the cost structure and improved profitability. The unanswered question that remains is how sustainable these economies will prove to be in the long run. The essential work of corporate services and oversight must go on at some irreducable level, and to some extent these cost savings were merely costs postponed. In later chapters the comparable experience of cost restructuring under a voluntary process is described, and it is seen to be substantially less abrupt and draconian. In Safeway, the harsh financial discipline imposed by the funding of the LBO left management with no choice.

The Structure of Constituency Claims

One of the most elusive aspects of the whole restructuring phenomenon is defining and documenting the nature and degree of long-term value creation. Indeed, there is room for a healthy debate as to whether restructuring, voluntary or involuntary, represents the creation of new value, the transfer of existing value (from one constituency to another), or even in some cases the destruction of value. My own conclusion is, probably all three. The field studies upon which this book is based have provided powerful examples of a major redistribution of the share of the wealth-creation process among new and old equity holders, debt holders, the work force, suppliers, and host communities.

The renegotiation of well-established long-term contracts, formal and informal, as has been previously remarked, is a particularly difficult process under normal circumstances, yet it may be the most critical element of renewing the competitive edge of an enterprise. It is also one which does not lend itself to arbitrary action by the ultimate corporate authority, as is true of most other restructuring options. Rather, it is a negotiated process between the corporation and each constituent interest, better suited to patient, experienced, professional managers.

However, there are occasions when events conspire to so empower one constituency over another that sudden and substantial redistribution of wealth takes place. Just such an event took place on December 31, 1985, when Foote Minerals, a subsidiary of Newmont Mining Corporation, closed its ferrosilicon plant in Graham, West Virginia. The case illustrates how restructuring creates opportunities lost and opportunities gained, the loss here being to the shareholders of Newmont Mining and its financially troubled subsidiary. It shows how the sustained gains that may result from restructuring constituent claims may be inaccessible to the troubled enterprise but are then captured by new owners whose negotiating position proves to be much stronger, with more options from which to choose.

The end product of Foote Mineral's Graham plant was used in foundries engaged in aluminum and steel manufacture. The metals industries are inherently cyclical, and in recent years ferrosilicon production in the United States had been subject to intense international competition from South Africa, Norway, and South America. For several years prior to 1985, Foote Minerals had been losing money in the modern but high-cost Graham plant. A labor contract with the United Steel Workers was up for renegotiation in 1983, and management sought major concessions. (At the same time, they were seeking, unsuccessfully, to gain power-rate concessions, since electric power and labor were the prime components of cost.) The union refused the concessions and went on strike. In December 1985, Newmont announced the permanent closing of the Graham plant and in the process took an $11 million write-off.

The Graham plant remained idle for two years without a viable opportunity to dispose of the property. At the time of its closing the plant, which employed 210 hourly workers and 50 salaried personnel, was the primary employer in an economically depressed county of West Virginia. When a group of employees sought to purchase the plant, the state offered a $4 million loan to assist a $23 million proposed funding, and the legislature passed a law exempting the plant from a business and occupational tax on electricity. However, the employees were unable to raise the equity funds.

In the fall of 1987, a firm called Renaissance Partners, Inc., in association with a regional investment banker, Farrell & Co., put together a turnkey leveraged buyout of the Graham plant to become American Alloys. The purchase price was $8 million, with only $1 million of cash up front. The plant was a modern facility with a replacement cost of $100 million and insurable value of $65 million. In selling the plant, Foote Minerals avoided a $2 million shutdown cost payable to the unionized employees under its existing labor agreement.

The ownership of the new enterprise was primarily in the hands of outside investors, though a 30% minority position was taken by an employee stock option plan (ESOP) to be paid for over time by payroll deductions. Management also had an equity position. At its inception the company was funded in excess of 95% with debt. At the end of its first year of operation, American Alloys had recorded a profit of $1.1 million. Where did this newfound value come from? Largely, I suggest, from a dramatic shift in the nature and priority of claims on the corporate value-added.

The following were key elements of the wealth transfer process:

1. the give-up of the potential value of the Graham plant by the shareholders of the former owner, Newmont Mining, to the new shareholders of American Alloys owing to Newmont's lack of a viable alternative. (Newmont subsequently sold Foote Minerals in 1987.) A secondary give-up by Newmont was in agreeing to finance most of the purchase price on very favorable terms.
2. the assumption of the risks of extreme leverage by various groups of lenders, including the state of West Virginia, for limited and in some cases very modest rates of return (10% interest rate for a West Virginia Industrial Corporation five-year note).
3. a five-year contract with Appalachian Power Company at a rate which reduced power costs to 23% below that paid by the former owner. (Electric power was historically 38% of the sales value of a ton of ferrosilicon.)

4. a new five-year labor contract with the United Steel Workers, which reduced wage and benefit costs from $20 an hour to $14 an hour, one dollar of which would go to the purchase of stock under the ESOP. This, combined with a reduction of required jobs, effectively reduced labor costs by 50%. Further, productivity was expected to benefit from the ESOP.
5. direct and indirect tax benefits under the ESOP, in part through lower borrowing rates for lenders that received a tax advantage. The new company also benefited from an exemption from state electricity taxes.

Thus the new American Alloys shareholders benefited from favorable concessions from former shareholders, bondholders and other lenders, suppliers, employees, and state and federal taxpayers. This enabled the new company to develop a viable cost structure upon which to compete successfully against domestic and foreign competitors, at least during its first five years of operation. It is admittedly an extreme example, and a function of the unique circumstances of the case: a depressed industry and local economy, an unprofitable subsidiary, and a work force with no place to go. However, it is precisely these shifts in bargaining power which permit a recontracting process that transfers benefits in favor of the ownership constituency. In Chapter 7, a less dramatic but more typical example of the restructuring of constituency claims is described in the case of Burlington Northern.

The Ultimate Payoff

The payoff from restructuring comes in different forms to different people. For management it is survival in office and the chance to shape a new corporate agenda. For employees it is the preservation of jobs and future income potential. For shareholders it is the preservation and enhancement of equity value. For the corporation as a whole it is the rebuilding of a secure revenue base with the potential for future profitability and growth.

The various elements of restructuring described and illustrated in this and the previous chapter come together in demonstrated, sustained improvement in return on investment, specifically return on equity or owner's investment. The three components are an improved profit margin on sales, a more efficient use of invested assets, and a more aggressive use of nonequity sources of funding. In the chapters dealing with the deterioration of financial performance in the 1960s and 1970s, primarily driven by organizational objectives, the evidence of decline was apparent. The success of a program of restructuring will be evident in a reversal of that trend. I use the experience of Household International to illustrate both the magnitude and the time frame of fundamental change in financial performance. Household's investment restructuring was outlined in Chapter 4. I now complete the picture.

In the 1970s Household International (then Household Finance) was vigorously pursuing unrestrained growth and diversification, prompting the company to say with pride that it served "eight out of ten families in the United States every year." Consecutive increases in aggregate earnings—and earnings per share—were the primary financial goal. In 1973, for example, the company reported an interruption in this growth—the first in 14 years—but hastened to reassure shareholders that they could look forward to a resumption of its prior earnings trend in 1974. (It should be noted that, as is commonly the case, this goal was made easier by the fact that the company regularly retained and reinvested 50% of these earnings.) A related goal was continuity and growth in dividends per share. In 1976 the company reported consecutive dividends for all 51 years since incorporation and *continuously increasing* annual cash dividends for the past 24 years. Growth in earnings per share and continuity in dividends were believed by the company to be the driving force behind the increasing market valuation of mature corporate equities.

In January 1977, D.C. Clark became president and continued as chief financial officer. His growing influence on corporate direction was reflected in the fact that the *Annual Report* for 1977 contained, for the first time, a reference to a new criterion: "a return on shareholders' average book equity of 15.4% compared with 13.9% in 1976." Clark did not become CEO until 1982, but before that date Household had publicly announced the following new set of corporate objectives:

1. to achieve an after-tax return on equity of 15% per annum
2. to maintain a balance of diversified businesses designed to achieve steady, balanced growth in revenues, earnings, and dividends
3. to attract and retain people of the highest caliber
4. to maintain a strong and conservative financial structure.

Undoubtedly stimulated by concurrent inflation and recession at the turn of the decade, Clark was beginning to restructure Household, particularly with respect to interest-sensitive financial services. The prior thrust for persistent absolute growth was to be replaced by a companywide standard focused on the to-be-attained ROE. Growth in EPS was then secondary. In 1981, a project was already under way to get a measure of ROE by division. Each division was to be assigned a capital structure by a nominal attribution of corporate debt appropriate to divisional risk. There was a strong effort to create a companywide ROE culture, and the word was getting around that unless every division met the 15% target it might not be retained. The reordering of priorities initiated by Donald Clark as CFO in 1977, and implemented by him as CEO beginning in 1982, reflected a shift in attention: (1) from organizational priorities to investor priorities, (2) from the corporate investment portfolio to the shareholders' investment portfolio, (3) from quantity (growth in absolute size) to quality (return per unit of invested capital).

The results of Household's restructuring are presented in Figures 5.1, 5.2, and 5.3, which show (1) return on sales (gross revenues), (2) return on assets (total invested capital), and (3) return on equity (at book value). The data begin with 1977, when Donald Clark became president and began to focus on ROE. In interpreting these data the reader is reminded that the profit margins and return on assets were fundamentally affected by the diversification into manufacturing and merchandising in the 1970s and the subsequent return to an exclusive focus on financial services in the 1980s. There is an obvious difference between the asset and liability structure, as well as the time profile of revenues, among these radically different industries.

The dramatic change in the refocusing and restructuring of Household is most apparent in Figure 5.1. The sustained downward trend in ROS ended in 1982 and became a strong upward trend, which persisted through 1988. By 1985, Household had surpassed both the S&P 500 index and the S&P personal finance industry index of ROS. However, in 1989 the company began to suffer the effects of a decline in the domestic and world economies, particularly from the deterioration in the domestic commercial real estate market. These trends were also apparent in the S&P 500 index.

The improvement in return on sales did not translate into a comparable improvement in return on assets, as Figure 5.2 makes plain. Except for a short rebound in ROA in 1983 and 1984, the downward trend apparent in the 1970s persisted throughout the entire period—a long-term trend also apparent in the S&P index. The shrinking of the asset base associated with the exit from manufacturing and mer-

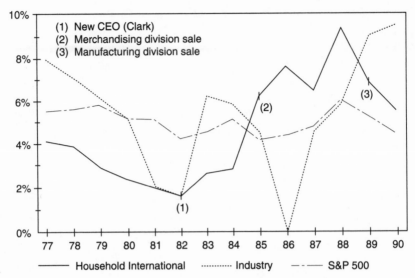

Figure 5.1 Household International Net Return on Sales

Source: Standard & Poor's COMPUSTAT.

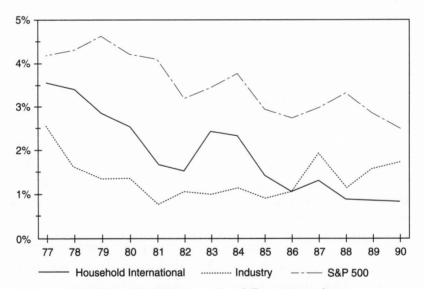

Figure 5.2 Household International Return on Assets

Source: Standard & Poor's COMPUSTAT.

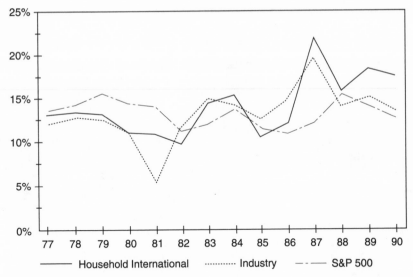

Figure 5.3   Household International Return on Equity

Source: Standard & Poor's COMPUSTAT.

chandising was offset by aggressive growth and diversification in the capital-intensive financial services industry. In contrast, the S&P personal financial services index shows an upward trend in ROA beginning in 1988. Such comparisons must be made with caution, however, in view of the differences in product-line mix from company to company.

Figure 5.3 shows return on shareholders' equity, the criterion Donald Clark introduced in 1977 as the primary measure for corporate financial performance. This ratio incorporates the third element of restructuring, changes in the funding mix of debt and equity. The historical record of ROE shows a clear change in the trend after 1982. Household surpassed the S&P 500 ROE index in 1986 and the S&P personal finance segment index in 1987. The contrast with return on assets was the result of a more aggressive use of debt leverage (debt-equity ratio: 2.7 times in 1982, 5.7 times in 1990) associated with expansion in financial services. (The increased risk was reflected in both a decline in bond rating and a rising equity "beta"—the index of stock volatility.)

Overall, the restructuring of Household International showed clear evidence of a turnaround in financial performance, as measured by the management's own standards. Clearly, there was a reversal of

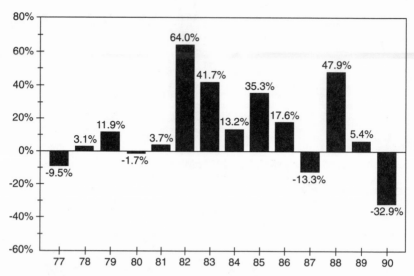

Figure 5.4 Household International Total Annual Return
to Shareholders

Note: 1989 and 1990 include three spin-offs: Eljer, Schwitzer, and Scotsman.
Source: Standard & Poor's COMPUSTAT.

the trend, which reached a low of 9.5% ROE in 1982 and subsequently averaged 15.7% for the years 1983 through 1990. The reader is reminded that in 1977, while he was CFO and president, Clark had set a target ROE of 15%. The turnaround coincided with the year in which Clark became CEO.

The ultimate test was how investors responded. That is depicted in Figure 5.4, showing total annual return to shareholders from the combination of dividends and capital gains, including spin-offs. The returns since 1982, obviously a substantial improvement over prior years, roughly coincide with the turnaround in ROE. Despite the poor performance in 1990, triggered by market concerns over Household's real estate portfolio, the average return for the years 1982 to 1990 inclusive was 18.6%, compared to the S&P 500 average total annual return of 18.4% for the same period.

Market returns are, of course, a function of many factors and cannot be directly linked to specific actions of management or indices of company performance. Nevertheless, it is clear that the 1980s restructuring of Household International was a time of strong and sustained investor confidence in the company's common stock and could justifiably be interpreted as approval of the actions taken.

The Process of Structural Change

CHAPTER 6

Alertness to Change:
General Mills, Inc.

Introduction to Part II

The purpose of Part II is to give the reader an in-depth acquaintance with the seamless evolution of corporate structure and strategy in the individual firm. It thus becomes apparent how the periodic restructuring, which every mature company has experienced, has its roots in the strategy and structure of the preceding period. It is also evident that the strategy and structure is a creature of its time and can be explained, if not justified, by the environmental forces then in place.

The three case histories provide a sampling of the divergent nature and influence of the internal governance process across the set of companies included in the study. The case of General Mills is an example of the traditional role of a chief executive, not only in setting the direction of corporate strategy and structure during his or her tenure, but also in having a strong if not dominant influence on the choice of successor. It is an instance of voluntary restructuring in its purest form.

The case of Burlington Northern (BN) illustrates the critical im-

An edited version of this chapter appeared in the *Journal of Financial Economics*, vol. 27, no. 1 (September 1990), pp. 117–141, and in the *Journal of Applied Corporate Finance*, vol. 4, no. 3 (Fall 1991), pp. 6–19.

portance of board intervention when the process of natural succession threatens to perpetuate a strategy at odds with environmental reality and to delay an increasingly urgent need for change. It also illustrates two other important issues. One is the opportune role of outside appointments to leadership when the ownership of outdated strategies is a burden to all inside candidates. This was also illustrated at certain points in the General Mills history. The other is the central problem BN faced in its railroad operations in the need to change fundamentally the structure of costs and revenues, a task which takes the time, patience, and persistence that only a professional manager can give.

The case of CPC International illustrates the impact of external intervention by a corporate "raider," the circumstances that created the potential for external intervention, and the manner in which incumbent management led a successful defense. These three cases span the full spectrum of voluntary and involuntary restructuring and of internal as well as external intervention.

Chapter Overview

Efficient and effective self-discipline is measured by the capacity of a mature corporate organization to adapt successfully to a changing economic environment without overt, adversarial intervention by one of its primary constituencies or by society. Frequent or widespread intervention by workers, investors, customers, regulatory agencies, or the judicial system is evidence of a serious breakdown of self-discipline and the potential loss of freedom and independence commonly attributed to a private enterprise system. A healthy system is one in which the governing authority recognizes the need for change, correctly identifies an appropriate response, and acts on it before the rising stresses of change trigger active intervention.

An example of effective self-discipline is to be seen in the evolution of General Mills since its incorporation in 1928, particularly in the transition from the post–World War II strategy and structure, which persisted through the 1970s, to a radical restructuring, which emerged in the 1980s. Since World War II, General Mills has in fact undergone two major restructurings. The first occurred following the end of the war when the company abandoned its founding concept of primary dependence on a national commodity market (flour) and aggressively pursued the markets for branded, packaged convenience foods. This strategy then evolved into extensive product-market diversification loosely linked by corporate expertise in the national distribution of branded, low-unit-price, high-turnover consumer goods. Founded on the objective of corporate independence from product- and capital-market risk, this strategy and its related financial structure persisted through the 1960s and 1970s.

Then, in the 1980s, another major restructuring occurred. It was driven by the conviction on the part of corporate leadership that the prior strategy was increasingly out of sync with investor perceptions of the best use of corporate resources. Recognizing that a general shift in investor attitudes was under way, generating pressure for change, management began to dismantle the diversification of the past two decades and to focus once again on packaged convenience foods and food-related services. Funds released by the shrinking of the invest- ment base were returned to the capital markets. The new General Mills not only had a much narrower product-market base but had also divested the financial reserves that had hitherto insulated the company from capital-market risk. As a result, the company had a renewed sensitivity—and vulnerability—to its capital and product- market environment.

Both major restructurings were accomplished through actions initiated within General Mills' internal governance system. The com- pany was widely regarded as well managed and conservative, an- chored in the stable culture of the Midwest, and there were no at- tempted takeovers to spur the process along. While conscious of the rising turmoil in corporate ownership as the 1980s progressed, the company was ahead of the wave and prepared for action as the oppor- tunity occurred. Leadership had passed from the founder's family early in the 1960s and a succession of CEOs, some insiders and some outsiders, followed with sufficient frequency that the opportunity to rethink direction on the order of once a decade was a natural and recurring event. It is this renewal process that we now proceed to examine in detail.

A History of Voluntary Restructuring: Prologue

General Mills began its corporate existence in 1928 as the instrument for restructuring the U.S. flour-milling industry from a series of regional mills into the world's largest miller of flour. In that year James Ford Bell, a Minneapolis entrepreneur and mill owner, organized the consolidation of 7 regional flour and feed mills into one company. Within 5 months General Mills incorporated 27 associated companies in 16 states. The unique attribute of the new company was the formation of a national marketing and distribution system for flour. This system would later serve as a base for aggressively advertised packaged consumer foods derived from grains, with the emphasis on convenience and ease of preparation.

The next 20 years were difficult ones for the new company. Barely under way, General Mills was confronted with the deep and prolonged depression of the 1930s. Annual sales volume in 1941 was $127 million, only $3 million more than it had been in 1929. World War II brought on the dislocations caused by the demands of war production. General Mills was thrust into manufacturing, among other things, such products as high-precision ordnance equipment. Although the war years more than doubled sales, net earnings increased by only 30%. Through 1946, net earnings had increased by a compound growth rate of only 3% per annum since 1929.

By 1952, Charles H. Bell, son of the founder, had assumed the presidency while his father continued to serve on the board. The younger Bell extended the strategy of unrelated diversification imposed by the war effort and, under a more decentralized management structure, broadened General Mills' involvement into small household appliances, military electronics, chemicals, and even, surprisingly, into two-man midget submarines and high-altitude balloons. At the same time he invested heavily in food research facilities and personnel. Concurrently, General Mills was experiencing heavy losses in formula (animal) feeds, and its core business was deteriorating owing to excess industry capacity. In a 1961 survey of the food industry, *Forbes* magazine ranked General Mills second to last. The financial results demonstrated that the company had lost its way. Between 1948 and 1958, sales increased 15% and employees 12% (in total), but net earnings fluctuated in a narrow band without any clear trend. Earnings per share in 1948 were $.49 and in 1958, $.50.

A major turning point occurred when Bell decided to strengthen the corporate management and provide for future leadership by going outside the company for his own replacement. He chose Edwin Rawlings, a four-star general, head of the U.S. Air Force Materiel Command and Bell's commanding officer in World War II. Rawlings was initially financial vice president, and two years later (1961) he became president. Bell moved up to chairman of the board and turned full operating responsibility over to Rawlings. Rawlings realized quickly that World War II had been a watershed in the economic and competitive environment of the company and that General Mills had failed to adjust. Foremost among the new competitive facts of life were (1) the declining per capita consumption of flour, as people upgraded their diets to include more meat, leading to razor-thin margins for bulk flour; (2) the skyrocketing demand for convenience foods; (3) the postwar baby boom; and (4) the diminishing prospects for the formula feed business, one of General Mills' original businesses. Too much of the company's financial and managerial resources was directed at businesses that were low return at best and had extremely limited growth potential.

The result of the Rawlings reassessment was the first major voluntary restructuring of General Mills. Its three central elements were, first, the divestiture of several unrelated or unprofitable businesses— electronics, formula feeds, and oil seeds. Second, Rawlings made a dramatic shift away from the origins of the company ("the world's largest flour mill") by closing 9 of 17 flour mills. This cut in half the portion of the revenue stream based on large-volume, low-margin commodity products. The company took an immediate hit in its forward momentum by giving up $200 million in sales volume and shrinking the work force by 29%. Third, and most important, Rawlings staked out a commitment to focused growth centered on branded, proprietary consumer foods and selected consumer nonfood businesses. Rawlings also sought to guide General Mills into faster-growing food areas. The implementation of these goals led to the acquisition of Tom's Foods (snacks) and Gorton (frozen fish), as well as Kenner Products (toys). Over the next eight years the share of corporate sales from consumer foods increased from 45% to 80%, and corporate earnings per share doubled.

That doubling reflected a change in financial goals initiated by Rawlings, which he summed up in a 1966 speech:

Proud as we were—and are—of our dividend record, we determined in the future to measure our progress to a great extent by earnings per share . . . Accent on dividends tends to produce a conservative attitude . . . Emphasis on earnings tends to produce a more aggressive forward looking attitude, including a willingness to accept risk in pursuit of growth.

The Origins of "The All-Weather Growth Company"

On December 31, 1968, Rawlings retired and chose James McFarland as his successor. McFarland had begun his career with the company 27 years earlier as a grain accountant and worked his way up the sales and merchandising side of the corporate ladder. It was McFarland who, 15 years later, unknowingly set the stage for the financial restructuring of the 1980s.

Starting from a vigorous base in consumer foods and a foundation in consumer nonfoods, McFarland guided the company down a course of aggressive growth and further diversification. At the time the stock market was valuing foods as a mature industry and gave these companies relatively low P/Es. McFarland expected to enhance the company's growth potential—and multiple—through further diversification and faster overall growth, but he planned to keep foods dominant in order to stabilize earnings. In a phrase that was to become a strategic mandate for both career employees and long-term financial investors, General Mills was to be "The All-Weather Growth Company," thus confirming a commitment to both growth *and* stability.

Rawlings had moved aggressively to position General Mills in the forefront of the growing market for branded, packaged convenience foods sold through supermarkets. The success of this strategy was manifest in a flow of funds from the product markets, which despite the continued growth potential was well beyond the available investment opportunities in foods alone. The new equity market of the 1970s played an insignificant role in the funding during this period of sustained growth, through 1983. There were no equity issues for cash and only modest, occasional distributions for acquisitions. Further, for most years, product-market flows—net of working capital needs—carried the major burden of new investment with only modest assistance from new debt capital.

Rather than distribute these excess funds to shareholders through a higher dividend payout, McFarland chose to surround the traditional core business with a cocoon of "related" business segments. This strategy had the appearance, if not the intent, of providing an independent internal capital market within which the core could evolve. The general shift in emphasis away from dividends to growth in earnings per share had the support of those shareholders who preferred capital gains, and management was only too happy to feed the corporate appetite for growth. In the case of General Mills, the operating rationale of the increasingly diverse product-market initiatives was the undisputed expertise of General Mills in the national marketing of consumer goods that had the following characteristics: (1) a

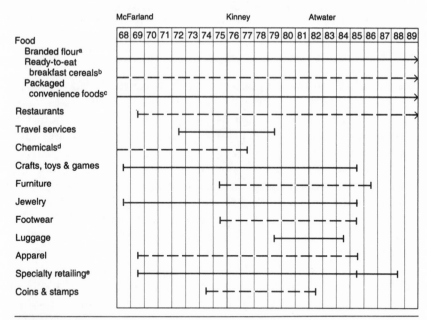

Figure 6.1 General Mills, Inc. Time Line of Diversification by Term of Chief Executive, 1968–1989

low price per unit, (2) a branded, proprietary name, and (3) repeat-purchase opportunities.

The pattern of diversification under McFarland is shown in Figure 6.1. The acquisition strategy included, among other things, markedly expanding the toys, games, and apparel areas and entering the specialty retailing, travel services, rare coins, and stamp businesses—all with a well-established, national-brand "franchise." This diversification was launched in 1968 and 1969 by a substantial infusion of funds from the capital markets, but from that point on was almost entirely funded by internal product-market flows. Self-sustaining growth, buttressed by a highly conservative debt policy, was the central funding strategy.

McFarland was described by his colleagues as "a food man through and through." However, he pursued a discipline of corporate self-evaluation to see that the company had the right businesses to meet its financial goals. He concluded that the company had to expand each of its existing businesses. Through all levels of the company, people were asked to identify growth strategies. Venture teams were formed to find new opportunities that eventually led to a spate of acquisitions. The incentive structure led some managers to count success by the number of deals completed. The exception was foods, where growth came primarily from internal research and development.

Management's test of a good strategy is good performance, regardless of the reasons for success. Certainly general prosperity, buoyant capital markets, and moderate inflation played their part during this period. To a management focused on internal indices of the variables over which it exercised control, the evidence on company performance was encouraging. During the McFarland era (1968–1975), sales increased at a compound growth rate of 14% annually and net earnings increased at a compound annual growth rate of 13.5%. Equally satisfying to management, General Mills' return on book equity was consistently outperforming both its industry peer group and the S&P 500. It all seemed to confirm the wisdom of the path chosen by McFarland and, particularly in the early years, the equity market appeared to give a strong vote of confidence. Between 1970 and 1972 the stock rose from $24 to $60 a share.

On a relative scale—relative to its past performance and to its industry competitors—General Mills demonstrated superior performance. On an absolute scale of maximum potential, however, warning signs were beginning to appear. In contrast to the Rawlings era, when return on sales had increased dramatically through an improvement in the sales mix, under McFarland it declined from 4.7% to 3.3%. Over this period, General Mills experienced low returns on its new acquisitions; elsewhere, returns were satisfactory. This was not surprising in view of the shift in leadership to a lifelong salesman whose instincts were to judge success primarily on the corporate sales scoreboard. While total asset turnover rose over the same period, inventory turnover declined dramatically, from 8.6 times to 4.4 times. This was obviously affected by a sharp change in product mix but also reflected management priorities: trading off efficient utilization of funds in favor of corporate strength, continuity, and defensive capability. Concurrent with these changes, liquidity ratios were rising and debt-equity ratios falling. Overall, the trend pointed to a decline in the percentage of total potential resources committed to active product-market investment and in the potential returns on resources actively employed. The promise of all-weather growth and corporate self-sufficiency came at a price.

Before passing judgment on McFarland and a growth strategy of diversification which, in the 1990s, appears misguided if not self-serving, the reader should bear in mind the organizational context of the time. As stated in Chapter 2, the corporate leaders of this period were young adults in the 1930s whose early business and personal lives were profoundly affected by the collapse of the capital markets during the Great Depression. This led them to be deeply skeptical of the public capital markets as a reliable source of personal or corporate funding, to avoid financial risk wherever possible, and to have an instinctive affinity for a strategy of self-sufficiency. It was natural for management to attribute the same values to "loyal" shareholders who, in an earlier era, looked to the company to serve the risk-reducing functions today being served increasingly by mutual fund managers. (Even as early as 1970, institutional investors held 65% of General Mills stock.)

It should also be remembered that management serves more than one master. Indeed, one of McFarland's predecessors had often gone on record in stating that "good people are the company's most important asset." To the investors of human capital—much less diversified and mobile than investors of financial capital—growth and stability are primary ingredients of a congenial working environment. In the light of these considerations, the McFarland strategy was a natural and, to him, rational response to the corporate environment as he knew it.

Consolidating the Gains, Assessing the Losses

When McFarland retired as chief executive in 1976, the board approved as his successor E. Robert Kinney, the first and only non-Midwesterner to head the company. Like General Rawlings, Kinney had achieved senior administrative responsibility before joining General Mills, which in 1968 inherited him as the chief executive of Gorton's Seafoods. In accordance with General Mills' custom of the time for most new members of executive management who came from operations, Kinney served a term as chief financial officer before becoming chief operating officer under McFarland.

The impact of the McFarland era had been dramatic. Between 1969 and 1976, sales volume tripled—from $885 million to $2.65 billion—as did earnings, and the employee count rose from 26,000 to 52,000. The effects of diversification on the relative importance of food processing are seen in the following figures:

	1968	1976
Food processing	90%	62%
Crafts, games, toys	6%	13%
Specialty retailing/fashion	0	14%
Restaurants	0	7%
Specialty chemicals	1%	4%
Other	3%	0
	100%	100%

Under Kinney, the era of aggressive diversification came to an end. He began a period of consolidation, which continued throughout his tenure as CEO. This had already been signaled by McFarland before he left office, and the choice of Kinney confirmed the desire to spend some time "digesting" and taking stock of the far-flung operations. For Kinney, it was important to slow down the acquisitions and get the earnings up. He worked hard to narrow the focus of growth and to improve investment returns. As an example, he cut back McFarland's venture teams to concentrate on fewer, more promising opportunities.

However, despite the change of administration and the opportunity to chart a new course, a radical shift seemed inappropriate. To Kinney, the stockholder interest meant managing the existing corporate resources more efficiently, a task he had begun as chief operating officer. Tightening corporate controls, Kinney initiated a working capital charge on operating managers. "Money goes where it's treated best" was the catch phrase. Kinney was aware that a sustained period of growth and profitability tended to mask mistakes and weaknesses that would be exposed in a less hospitable economic environment.

It is not easy to discipline a large diverse organization when it is doing extremely well. Although the customary internal standard was return on (book) assets employed, the ultimate management standard was return on book equity, and by this standard steady progress was being made. In only one year during Kinney's six-year tenure did the results fail to match or surpass the target and to demonstrate steady improvement. This evidence confirmed the general impression among analysts and the business press that General Mills was an exceptionally well-managed company. Commenting on Kinney's appointment as the new CEO of General Mills, *Fortune* magazine said: "Kinney will do well to equal his predecessor's record. During the past decade, General Mills has more than doubled its earnings per share and provided investors with a total return of 9.7 percent a year—nearly twice the industry median."[1] (The compound annualized return for the S&P 500 for the period 1966–1975 was 3.27%.)[2]

In a similar vein, a 1981 Merrill Lynch analysts' report expressed the following opinion:

General Mills is, in our view, one of the best structured, best managed companies in the packaged food industry. Ensconced in an industry where real growth in the future is destined to approximate population growth, General Mills has: a) been an industry leader in the important area of innovative product development in higher-margined packaged foods; b) developed a textbook success in full-service restaurant chains—Red Lobster Inns of America; and c) successfully diversified over the past decade into higher growth fields such as fashion, specialty retailing and toys.[3]

One important fact was troubling, however. The equity market's response to McFarland in the early years had been ecstatic, pushing the price-earnings ratio in 1973 to a peak of 22 and putting the company well ahead of both its industry and the S&P ratios. However, since 1973 the P/E ratios for General Mills and the market as a whole had been declining, and even worse, the gap between General Mills and the market had been gradually closing. General Mills' market-to-book ratio had been 3.1 in 1973; by 1979 it was 1.4. This disturbing trend did not escape management's attention but could, for a time, be explained away as a general market phenomenon, one over which individual management had, apparently, little control.

Through the late 1970s Kinney continued "balanced diversification," with modest further acquisitions. At the same time Kinney

[1] *Fortune*, July 1976, p. 27.

[2] R.G. Ibbotson and R.A. Sinquefield, *Stocks, Bonds, Bills and Inflation: The Past and the Future* (Charlottesville, Va.: Financial Analysts Research Foundation, 1976).

[3] *The Wall Street Transcript*, March 9, 1981, p. 60832.

and his chief operating officer, Bruce Atwater, a 23-year veteran of the consumer foods division, began a review of the corporate legacy they had inherited, particularly market positions in 13 different industries. The competitive strength of each subsidiary varied greatly and so did top management's confidence in the capacity of each unit to meet and beat its immediate rivals in the marketplace.

The first hint of a rethinking of the corporate structure came in August 1977, when General Mills sold General Mills Chemicals. The specialty chemicals business, an isolated operation constantly in need of new funding, was cyclical and capital intensive, and lacked scale and unique expertise. However, this move released a modest $72 million in net cash proceeds and was perceived as merely tidying up around the edges. In 1978, General Mills celebrated its fiftieth anniversary and reaffirmed its continued evolution from a commodity-based food company to one of "balanced diversification." To all appearances the strategy that had been in place for two decades was still secure.

New Leadership, New Environment

In 1981, Atwater became chief executive officer, succeeding Kinney, with whom he had worked closely throughout Kinney's entire tenure. A year later Kinney stepped down as chairman. (He retired from the board in 1985.) In 1980, Kinney and Atwater, with active encouragement from the board, had made an unusual selection for the next chief financial officer, choosing Mark Willes, president of the Federal Reserve Bank of Minneapolis. Hitherto the office of CFO had been a designated training ground for the senior general management circle and, as such, meant that senior officers were sensitized to the financial aspects of management. However, it was an internal, corporate view of the world. For the first time, the CFO would bring a strong external capital-market perspective to financial decision making. (Willes became president of General Mills in 1986 and vice chairman in 1991.) The appointment showed a perceptive sensitivity to a changing environment.

The naming of Atwater and Willes is an example of how an informed and attentive board can be influential at critical turning points. The board was actively involved in both these key appointments.

No major internal or external crisis occurred in the late 1970s and early 1980s in General Mills' immediate environment to justify a radical change of strategy. Thus it might appear that the quiet reexamination of the existing strategy and structure, which had begun with Kinney and continued with Atwater, may have been solely a function of the particular experiences, preferences, and values of the incumbent CEO. No doubt these were important. However, there were internal and external pressures building, which threatened to break apart the uneasy coexistence of the diverse products, markets, funds flows, and management cultures that made up the company. Among these lurking problems were:

- The reality that the growth and stability promised by the long-established corporate strategy was unevenly distributed across industries and products. Market share varied greatly and some product lines, notably games, toys, and fashion, were subject to sharp cyclical swings.
- The burden of meeting aggressive earnings goals rested primarily on the food lines, whose returns were consistently high. This prompted some resentment, as reflected in the wry comment that what the all-weather growth strategy really meant was, in the words of one executive, "The food groups will bail you out if you get in trouble."
- It was difficult to manage and monitor performance across industries with large cultural differences: mass-distribution foods versus fashion clothing versus the toy and game fads.
- The stock market was increasingly disenchanted with food companies and what it perceived to be General Mills' unfocused diversification. It was necessary for General Mills, as for many other companies, to run harder and harder to stay in place in overall market valuation.

Under Kinney's leadership, the first step toward restructuring had been taken: along with the moves to consolidate rather than further extend diversification, there was a distinct shift of emphasis from growth by acquisition to growth by internal development. Most capital expenditures during 1979–1981 were committed to consumer foods and restaurants. In 1981, the company announced that it would double capital expenditures over the next five years and that 75% of the budget would be spent on consumer foods and restaurants, a clear indicator of rededication to the traditional core.

Soon after their appointment to corporate leadership, Atwater

and Willes sought objective evidence on General Mills' performance—not as measured by its own past history, as is often the case
for an industry leader, but as measured by a marketwide reference
group. For this purpose they began a search among 6,000 publicly
traded companies for a set of companies "like General Mills." They
focused particularly on companies with (1) an ROE in excess of 19%,
(2) steady earnings growth, (3) over half a billion in assets, and (4)
low debt-equity ratios.

This population quickly collapsed to 88 companies that appeared
to have these characteristics, upon which further attention focused.
These data confirmed management's suspicions that the more diversified the company, the more "average" the performance. (After all,
the ultimate of diversification *is* the market average.) In contrast, most
leading performers—in fact, two-thirds of the 88, including many
of the largest—were concentrated in one or two industries. Only 5
companies were in 5 or more industries, as was true of General Mills.

The study also extended to the earnings performance of the industries in which General Mills then competed. This led the company
to reclassify and track its portfolio differently. A new interpretation
of "balance" had emerged—one no longer based on product markets
but on financial performance designed to produce and sustain growth
and superior ROE concurrently.

The Implementation of Voluntary Restructuring

The restructuring of the General Mills all-weather growth
company of the 1960s and 1970s took several years to emerge into
public view. The first phase of the restructuring of the 1980s shifted
away from growth by acquisition to growth based on internal investment, particularly in consumer foods and restaurants. The second
phase was the consolidation of the many industry segments into five
major core product groups: consumer foods, restaurants, toys, fashion, and specialty retailing.

For a time the all-weather-growth-company image was invoked
to convey a continuing commitment to all components and to multiple
corporate constituencies. However, the obvious effort to define the
long-term core of the business turned an uncomfortable spotlight on
a number of industry fragments, drawn into the corporate family at
the height of the expansion phase, around the issue of "fit": scale,
competitive advantage, consistency of performance, and growth po-

tential. Chemicals had already gone and gradually other bits and pieces disappeared: travel, luggage, coins and stamps, wallpaper, and some furniture operations.

Many studies of restructuring focus on the role of external pressures, particularly the threat of takeover, in precipitating the change. However, in the case of General Mills, it was the *internal* environmental pressures that dictated change. These were (1) the persistent clash of cultures between the traditional product-line managers and many of the newer "immigrants" from alien product markets and the difficulty of maintaining effective corporate oversight; (2) the resentment at persistent cash-flow subsidies going to the new "growth" segments; and (3) the friction caused by perceived inequality in the contribution to and rewards from corporate performance. It was only later in the decade, when the takeover environment for larger corporations heated up, that the external pressures—though not directed specifically at General Mills—began to show. (General Mills adopted antitakeover provisions in 1985.) No one can say to what extent the *pace* of change may have been accelerated because of these environmental forces.

As the restructuring of the 1980s began to emerge, it was accompanied by an important change in the management incentive system. In 1981, Atwater replaced a long-standing incentive system based solely on growth in earnings per share with a new incentive system equally balanced between growth in EPS and return on equity. The ROE goal was to be in the top quartile of the S&P 500 companies. The company had talked return on equity for years but acted as if sustained growth in earnings per share was the dominant concern of shareholders and a sufficient measure of fulfillment of the shareholder responsibility. Splitting the focus equally between growth and return on equity was a clear and unequivocal signal that the chief executive cared as much about superior returns on shareholder investment as he did about corporate continuity and growth. That major shift of emphasis prepared the ground for the changes to come.

With the corporate portfolio down to five industries, there was some remaining ambivalence regarding further reduction in the number of product markets. The 1984 long-range plan, presented to the board in April 1983, noted that the company was starting to explore the potential of a sixth area. Three factors drove this research: (1) increasing cash generation, (2) the possibility that a new related area was capable of growing faster than the corporation as a whole, and (3) doubts concerning the ability of existing groups to meet corporate targets for return on investment.

Despite the lingering appeal of an expanding corporate investment horizon, by late 1983 the stage was set for the beginning of the third phase of restructuring: a frontal attack on the concept of balanced diversity. The 1982 pre-tax return on assets shows the uneven performance across divisions.

Consumer foods	30.5%
Fashion	29.7%
Toys	19.7%
Restaurants	18.1%
Specialty retailing	2.0% (estimated)[4]

The first four were reported as performing in the upper quartile of their industries. The fifth segment, specialty retailing, had been struggling for several years despite a couple of star performers.

Beginning in the fall of 1984, fashion and then toys experienced a serious cyclical downturn. In 1982–1983, the fashion and toy groups accounted for 35% of corporate earnings. In 1984, the bottom fell out of the preppy craze and the consumer electronic toy markets. Operating return on assets for fashion fell from 29% in 1982 to 12% in 1984, and for toys from 23% in 1983 to 13% in 1984. It was an ideal time for management to confront the drag these operations were imposing on the consumer foods core—though not the ideal time to sell. In January 1985, General Mills announced it would explore the disposition of the entire toy and fashion segments, as well as some specialty retailing units The plan of divestment was implemented in November 1985 by a "spin-off"—the creation of two independent companies, Kenner Parker Toys Inc. and Crystal Brands Inc., the stock of which was distributed to General Mills shareholders.

Internal discussion at this time revolved around the possibility of exiting all nonfood businesses. Rather than exiting specialty retailing, management decided to try to build its scale and management capability. Two years down the road, management would conclude that it had to increase the scale to reach a critical mass level or get out. Since General Mills was having difficulty building depth in management, it chose to complete the previously discussed divestiture—at a large profit. The planned refocusing was completed in May 1988 with the sale of the remaining specialty retailing businesses: Talbots to JUSCO Co., Ltd. (Japan), and Eddie Bauer to Spiegel Inc. for combined

[4] Alan S. Greditor, *Drexel Burnham Lambert Analyst Report*, June 19, 1985, p. 16.

gross proceeds of $585 million. These sales were the final steps in a transformation of General Mills, which had begun 12 years earlier under the Kinney-Atwater administration.

In its simplest terms, the shedding of activities that had cyclical and inferior ROEs could be expected to raise the corporate average ROE and improve the predictability of EPS. However, there was a short-term problem of replacing lost earnings. A setback in earnings per share, however temporary, creates market concerns that management may not be able to fully allay. In earlier years, when the company was perceived as the portfolio within which long-term, loyal shareholders achieved superior returns, liquid funds could justifiably be held to await an appropriate investment opportunity. However, in that era of vigilant and distrustful fund managers, the prudent action was to return the funds to the capital markets via the repurchase of common stock. The tradition of a highly conservative capital structure could belatedly be used to good advantage. The stock repurchase plan began in 1980, and by 1988 an amount equivalent to 27% of the outstanding common stock had been retired without adversely affecting the company's credit rating.

Corporate Transformation and Market Response

In reviewing a full restructuring cycle that had spanned almost three decades and brought the company full circle by restoring consumer foods to a position of dominance in the corporate revenue stream (72% of sales, 82% of operating profits), it is important to note the extent to which the core of the enterprise had been transformed. Certainly, a unique feature of the General Mills enterprise—the production and distribution of packaged convenience foods—was then, and is still, a highly profitable and stable business. Over the years there has been substantial extension and diversification of the product lines within consumer foods, as seen in Table 6.1. In addition, the retention and expansion of the restaurant business was viewed as a natural extension of consumer foods that were increasingly consumed outside the home. It is the current position of management that these two areas of operation provide ample opportunity for growth and superior rates of return.

In retrospect, it took Atwater four years to confirm the evidence and lay the groundwork on the need for change, and three years to execute the full restructuring. The results were dramatic.

Table 6.1 General Mills, Inc. Major Growth Businesses, 1988

	Year Entered Market	1988 Retail Sales ($ millions)	Current Market Share	Current Market Position
Frozen seafood	1968	$ 960	25%	£1
Yogurt	1977	1,150	19	2
Fruit snacks	1982	310	50	1
Frozen novelties	1986	1,620	6	3
Microwave popcorn	1986	400	18	2
Single-serving fruit drinks	1987	400	—	1[a]

[a] Available in limited markets.

Source: Company annual reports.

- Sales declined from a historic high of $5.6 billion in 1984 to a low of $4.2 billion in 1985, from which they then recovered to $5.6 billion in 1989.
- The number of employees declined from a high of 81,000 in 1983 to a low of 62,000 in 1986, rising again to 84,000 in 1989.
- Inventory turnover increased from a low of 4.8 times in 1983 to 7.9 times in 1989.
- The liquidity index declined from a high of 24% in 1981 to a low of 1% in 1989 (the index is defined as excess cash plus unused debt capacity as a percentage of total assets).
- The debt-to-equity ratio rose from a low of 27% in 1982 to 74% in 1989.
- Return on equity increased from 16.7% in 1980 to an incredible 56.6% in 1989.

General Mills once again placed a wide gap between itself and the S&P 500. The overall equity market response to these most recent changes was clear and positive, as seen in the data on growth rates in market value in Figure 6.2. To consider this response in a broader historical perspective, it is helpful to divide the last two decades into eras of corporate leadership. In the McFarland era, General Mills' performance dominated all rivals in the growth rate of the value of its equity, though it weakened in the second half of his incumbency. In the Kinney era, General Mills' performance strengthened, but fell behind its industry and the S&P 500. In the early part of the Atwater era, the company again pulled ahead of the S&P 500, but lagged the industry as it positioned itself for restructuring. In the final period, in which major restructuring was implemented, General Mills once

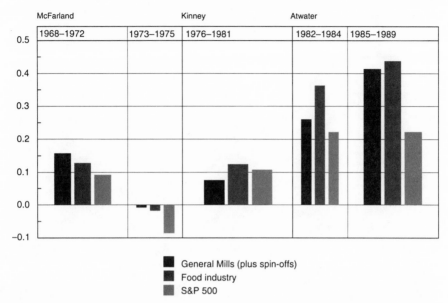

Figure 6.2   Average Annual Growth Rate of Value of One Unit of Stock of General Mills, the Food Industry, and the S&P 500 During 1968–1989*

*Market prices at calendar year end; growth in value during a period is measured by adding capital gains, dividends received, and, for General Mills, the ending market value of fractional interests in subsidiaries spun off (Crystal Brands and Kenner Parker, during the period 1985– 1989).

Source: Standard & Poor's COMPUSTAT.

again matched the phenomenal growth of the food industry and out-paced the S&P 500 stock performance.

Figure 6.3, showing price-earnings ratios, provides another view of the equity market response to General Mills' performance from a somewhat different perspective. Through 1971, General Mills was relatively indistinguishable from the pack. In 1972 and 1973, it pulled clearly ahead, where it remained through 1979 for the S&P 500 and through 1981 for the industry group. From 1980 to 1984, the company multiple was relatively indistinguishable from its capital-market competition. Then, in 1985, it soared again to dominate the industry and market averages by a wide margin. The latest decision to restructure General Mills appeared to be firmly supported by its stockholders.

These data reflect the perspective of career management accus-

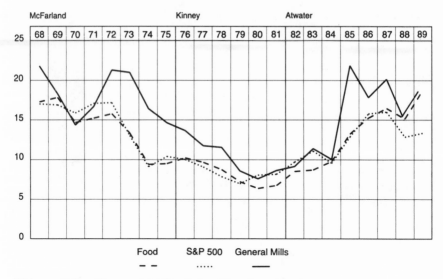

Figure 6.3   General Mills Price-Earnings Ratio

Sources: General Mills: Moody's Industrial Manuals (1968–1969) and Standard & Poor's COMPUSTAT (1970–1989); food industry and S&P 500: S&P *Analyst's Handbook*.

tomed to viewing corporate performance against the template of a series of five-year strategic planning cycles. Another viewpoint is that of the professional investor who is the recipient of fragments of information about evolving corporate strategies to which there are both an instantaneous and a cumulative response. A study of market-adjusted returns[5] around announcement dates of major events during periods dominated by either an acquisition/diversification or divestiture/restructuring strategy produces some interesting results.

In reviewing these data over the past three decades, one sees clearly that the market response to management's individual actions is not at all clear, with one major exception to be noted in a moment. Overall, both acquisitions and divestitures registered small positive market-adjusted returns. With respect to core versus noncore subsidiaries, the market appeared to favor expansion of the core of consumer foods and restaurants. If CEOs tracked the daily market polls—which, of course, they didn't—both Rawlings and McFarland would have taken comfort from the positive, if modest, response to their

[5] Market-adjusted returns are the increase or decrease in the value of General Mills stock less the corresponding increase or decrease in the Standard & Poor's 500 market index.

announcements regarding the evolving all-weather-growth strategy. Kinney, on the other hand, would have sensed mixed signals and general market irritation with almost any decision, since there appeared to be a negative response to both further acquisitions and divestitures.

Only at the end of the two decades do we detect a signal that could not be mistaken. When, on January 28, 1985, Atwater announced the decision to divest the toy and fashion groups, the two-day market-adjusted return was an astounding 12.85% increase. The response on January 7, 1988, when the sale of Talbots and Eddie Bauer was announced, was another 4% increase. There could be no doubt in Atwater's mind that he had done the right thing.

CHAPTER 7

Commitment to Change:
Burlington Northern Inc.

Chapter Overview

Chapter 3 described the circumstances under which Richard Bressler was appointed chief executive of Burlington Northern in June 1980. BN was in the process of merging with the St. Louis, San Francisco Railroad—the Frisco—to form the nation's largest railroad. In addition, it owned extensive and diversified natural resources, which had remained relatively undeveloped. Bressler, the first nonrailroader to run BN, was selected for his experience and expertise in managing resource-based companies and for his command of financial management. (Immediately prior to the BN appointment, he was executive vice president, Atlantic Richfield, and had been at one time chief financial officer of American Airlines.) BN needed radical restructuring—it had a return on assets of only 4% in 1979—and it was clearly the hope and intent of the board that the new appointment would improve the profitability of the railroad and release more of the value locked away in the undeveloped natural resources.

In a sense, Bressler's appointment was an internally conceived and executed "takeover," having many of the characteristics normally attributed to corporate raiders with their single-minded dedication to dramatic improvement in return to the equity holder. Bressler's

personality was in sharp contrast to that of his predecessor, Lou
Menk, who was close to the railroad people with whom he had spent
his life, outgoing, and gregarious. Bressler, inescapably the "outsider," was perceived as aloof, impersonal, and private. The shock
waves were not long in coming.

Within the year after taking office, Bressler moved BN's corporate headquarters from its historical base in St. Paul, Minnesota, to
Seattle. Operating headquarters of major railroad and natural resource divisions (oil and gas, coal, timber, real estate) were later dispersed to various parts of the country under new corporate leaders,
many of whom were brought in from other business enterprises. Each
division was set the task of realizing its full ROI potential through
specific financial goals and incentives. A key component of the strategy was uncoupling the operations of the railroad and natural resources, which historically had been bound together by long-term
debt contracts designed by J.P. Morgan and issued before the turn
of the century (1896) to assure maximum security for railroad bondholders.

Over the next decade, Bressler and his senior management
worked assiduously to

1. achieve a competitive return on investment in the railroad by
   aggressive marketing, cost control, and economy in the use of
   investment.
2. exploit the natural resource base for profitable development and
   increased scale of investment, ultimately to achieve parity with
   rail revenues.
3. have the freedom for investable capital to flow wherever prospective risk-adjusted returns were best.
4. focus corporate priorities on maximum value enhancement for
   equity holders.

The relatively simple and straightforward initial strategic plan
was to build up the natural resources revenue base to the point where
it could be a powerful financial tool in rationalizing the railroad. At
the core of the cost structure of the railroad was the considerable
economic and political power of the operating unions, which were
dedicated to preserving jobs, wages, and fringe benefits achieved over
the years of legislated and regulated negotiation. If BN had ultimately
to face a long strike in order to break the union control of the cost
structure, it needed a large war chest. Resources would provide those
funds.

The restructuring of the BN railroad was a long, slow, and difficult task. There were a number of major setbacks along the way arising from unexpected changes in the world and U.S. economies, in legislation, regulation, and court action, and in the response of communities, customers, competitors, and the organized work force. Despite this, however, there was gradual and significant improvement in the profitability of the rail operations.

On a parallel track, Bressler moved to expand the resources operation. In 1982 he initiated an unsolicited tender offer for El Paso Natural Gas Co. Other acquisitions followed. Thus the revenue potential from the operation of resource-based companies was greatly increased.

A critical component of better asset management in BN was the ability to transfer resources across the organization in search of product-market investments with highest return. This was facilitated by the formation of a holding company within which each operating division had greater autonomy in the use of resources. It was also facilitated by relief from the 1896 bond covenants directing that capital released from exploitation of natural resources be invested in the railroad. This was finally accomplished in November 1987. By these means excess funds owned by the railroad could be redirected for investment in the resource operations.

As the decade progressed, Bressler found that despite innovative and aggressive efforts to raise the ROI of the rail operation, each initiative ultimately reached a dead end. The crowning blow was the refusal of the courts to deny to the unions the right of secondary boycotts. As a result, any BN strike would soon spread to other railroads and immediately become a national political football. The grand strategy of a natural resource war chest to withstand a showdown strike by the operating unions was thereby voided.

As Bressler approached the end of his self-imposed decade of tenure in office, he conceded to himself that he was not going to achieve the level of return on the railroad that would in his mind justify a stand-alone long-term investment. Therefore, as his final act he would exercise Solomonic judgment and split the company in two, forming Burlington Resources Inc. and spinning off the ownership of its assets to the shareholders of BN Inc. Hence the value of each component—the natural resources and the railroad—could reach its own level and its own family of investors in the marketplace and, it was hoped, the sum of the parts would be worth more than the whole. This was finally accomplished in October 1988, when the board of directors approved the spin-off.

These events, which are chronicled in this chapter, illustrate the inherent capability of corporate self-government to confront and aggressively pursue major restructuring without the discipline of overt market intervention. They also illustrate vividly the time frame of turnaround: a full two decades before one strategy had run its course and a successful strategic renewal could be effected. It is a sobering lesson in the need for patience to accompany the national commitment to self-governance within a free enterprise system.

Setting the Stage

In June 1980, Burlington Northern was for the first time in its history headed by a man with no experience or prior association with railroads. To an industry steeped in tradition, it was a hell of a way to run a railroad. However, Richard Bressler was chosen by his predecessor, Lou Menk, himself a lifelong railroad man, precisely because he would be distanced from the values, traditions, priorities, and commitments of those who knew no other world than railroading. Bressler brought two principal assets to BN leadership: operating experience with resource-based enterprises and financial expertise. He also brought to corporate leadership an attitude that was intensely focused on gaining a competitive return on shareholder investment.

The shareholders of BN had fared poorly over the previous decade. The 1970s return on equity had averaged 4.3% while riskless U.S. Treasury bills earned 6.3%. In hindsight, the reasons were obvious. In an era when railroads were managed as a public trust, law, regulation, politics, and even bond contracts conspired to force reinvestment of all corporate funds for improved rail service with little regard for competitive equity returns. These results are therefore not too surprising.

During the 1970s, Menk had seized on what he believed to be a unique opportunity for BN. Its land ownership and rail location gave it a monopoly on access to the vast reserves of low-sulfur coal in the Powder River Basin along the Wyoming-Montana border. These resources appeared to present the opportunity of the century in response to OPEC's sudden grab for higher-priced oil. BN's response was to invest over $2 billion in new roadbed, facilities, and equipment for the highly efficient unit trains—typically 100 cars—that were to carry the coal to midwestern and Gulf Coast public utilities. Unstable world events and the inability of the U.S. government to implement a consistent long-term strategy of energy independence conspired to undermine Menk's strategy for the railroad.

By the time of his retirement, Menk was deeply disappointed in the financial results of the railroad and, in an act of unusual self-denial, agreed with his board that they should make a radical departure from tradition by appointing a nonrail chief executive dedicated to the restoration of investor confidence who would put return on investment before all else.

In response to this mandate, Bressler had a clear plan of action and wasted no time in making his ideas known to the organization and the business press. He told his senior colleagues that he would commit the next 10 years—no more—to revitalizing BN. It was a two-track strategy. He would undertake to break the management of natural resources loose from its traditional role as a secondary source of funding and creditworthiness for the railroad to become a major independent profit center and value generator for shareholders. In doing so, he planned to supplement the resources currently owned by BN with complementary acquisitions. His goal, he announced, was to make resources equal to the railroad in economic importance to the corporation by the end of the decade.

At the same time, Bressler intended to launch a frontal attack on the cost and revenue structure of the railroad to make it substantially more efficient and profitable. In this, he had the advantage that his predecessor had absorbed the worst of the inevitable dilution of ROI associated with a major upgrade of invested capital. It was now the profit and loss statement that demanded drastic restructuring. Bressler reasoned that to implement it—and particularly to take on the inevitable union opposition—he needed an independent source of funding, which the buildup of natural resources would provide. Standing alone, the railroad was highly vulnerable to an extended rail strike and the associated political and community pressure to compromise or give in.

Most new CEOs, particularly those who arrive from the outside, take several months to familiarize themselves with the facts regarding business operations and performance and to take the measure of existing management. Bressler behaved as if familiarity would be a hindrance, not a help. In a major move of both symbolic and practical significance, he disbanded the corporate headquarters in St. Paul in August 1981, relocating it to Seattle with a much smaller staff, thus walking away from the old railroad bureaucracy. For the time being, the operating divisions' headquarters, in particular the railroad, were left in St. Paul.

In May 1981, Bressler had taken a second and more significant step. He formed Burlington Northern Inc. as a holding company for the equity stock in eight independent operating subsidiaries: the railroad, the air freight company, trucking, forest management, forest products manufacturing, oil and gas, coal and minerals, and land and real estate. The holding company concept had several advantages.

1. It produced legal and operational separation among distinctively different product-market entities.
2. It consequently made it easier to focus on maximizing the unique profit potential of each.
3. It allowed for a clearer definition of management responsibility for performance.
4. It provided a mechanism for funds to be transferred across the system in search of the best return on investment.
5. It made it possible for the holding company to raise public equity and invest where needed.

Bressler's management style was to hire new chief executives for the subsidiaries from other successful companies in the same line of business, provide strong financial incentives based on profit performance, decentralize authority and responsibility, and give each leader the chance to succeed or fail—and be replaced. He encouraged geographic dispersion of headquarters. "You pick good people and get out of their way. If you are physically separated you don't get on each other's nerves from constant contact."

Developing Natural Resources

Under Lou Menk, resources management was in the hands of railroad men. In 1980, the person with overall responsibility for resources was a taciturn man who was reluctant to discuss his management objectives with Bressler. After considerable pressure, he finally explained that his aim was to minimize the cash flow from resources, because "it would only be squandered by railroad management." The primary strategy was to farm out the use of owned resources on terms that yielded only modest returns to BN.

The primary obstacle to more aggressive and independent management was the deeply entrenched belief that resources existed to support the railroad operation. This mentality had a valid historical foundation. At a time of financial difficulty (1896), BN's predecessor company, Northern Pacific, had negotiated two bond series, one of which was a 150-year bond due 2047, bearing 3% interest, with the covenant that any proceeds realized from the sale of the resources must be reinvested in the railroad. (The 1890s, like the 1980s, fostered a back-to-the-core investment mentality.)

Bressler tried on a number of occasions to renegotiate the loan contracts but was unsuccessful. The resistance from the insurance companies holding the bonds arose from the fact that it would force recognition on the books of grossly overstated market value of a large category of bonds carried at par with coupon rates well below current market. Finally, in November 1987, the federal courts ruled that BN could pay a $35 million premium to free up 4.3 million acres of land from collateral on the bonds. It took seven years to put in place one small but vital piece of the puzzle.

From the beginning, Bressler set out to make oil and gas exploration and transportation the centerpiece of the resources strategy. The plan was announced publicly in January 1982. Bressler began a search for oil and gas companies that might be acquired on favorable terms to add economies of scale to BN's existing properties. At the same time he began the accumulation of cash reserves to finance purchases, augmented by an unused $100 million bank line of credit. This cash reserve was increased in 1982 by the sale of BN Air Freight to the Pittston Company for $177 million. At the time, one analyst called this stupidity at its peak, reasoning that it was the most successful and profitable part of the BN transportation system. However, a major purchase of aircraft loomed as a necessary move in a highly competitive industry, and Bressler had other uses for the money in mind. In retrospect, Pittston discovered that it had overpaid for the business and proceeded to lose money for several years.

After considering a number of alternatives for acquisition, Bressler set his sights on El Paso Natural Gas. El Paso operated a natural gas pipeline from Texas to California which supplied 50% of California's natural gas consumption, was also engaged in oil and gas exploration, and had substantial reserves of gas. The company was then in a seriously weakened and overleveraged financial condition owing primarily to a disastrous contract with Algeria to produce and transport LNG to the United States. The result was a $365 million (after-tax) write-off (40% of El Paso's equity). In the midst of these difficulties (December 1982), Bressler launched a takeover bid. In an all-cash tender offer he picked up 48% of the common equity for $621 million. Twelve months later, BN acquired the balance of the stock for an additional $681 million in cash and stock. At $24 a share it was an aggressive price. Again, analysts expressed mixed reactions, fearing that Bressler had overpaid for a troubled company and an uncertain payoff. As part of the integration of El Paso into BN's oil and gas operations, Travis Petty, former CEO of El Paso, became vice chairman and a director of BN.

Two years later (1985), BN initiated a second takeover, that of Southland Royalty Company, an oil exploration and production operation. Southland was acquired for $695 million, all cash, at a price analysts considered reasonable. Its operations, along with El Paso's exploration and production operations, were merged into Meridian Oil.

However, Bressler's successful implementation of his oil and gas strategy was plagued by events beyond his control. Since 1980, crude oil prices had been gradually slipping, having reached $27 a barrel when BN acquired Southland. In 1986, oil prices collapsed, falling to a low of $8 a barrel in July.[1] A second shock to the strategy was the 1985 ruling of the Federal Energy Regulatory Commission forcing gas pipelines to honor long-term take-or-pay contracts with suppliers while releasing pipeline customers from purchase commitments to take advantage of lower spot prices.

These events hit BN's financial statements in 1986. Concurrently, BN chose that year to revise accounting methods and write down assets to provide a more realistic base going forward. A one-time special charge of $957 million ($802 million after tax) included a write-off of $352 million of rail equipment and a write-down of $605 million of oil and gas property values. The bottom line was a 1986 oil and gas operating loss of $586 million and a corporate after-tax loss of $860 million, of which $336 million was attributable to the railroad. On the positive side, operating income from natural gas operations was $295 million, down from a 1985 peak of $316 million. El Paso continued to be a primary cash-flow generator.

Working on the Railroad

Difficult as it was to implement an aggressive and successful natural resource strategy for BN as one of the two prongs directed toward improved corporate financial performance, by far the more

---

[1]Gilbert Jenkins, ed., *Oil Economists' Handbook*, 5th ed., vol. I (Ref: HD 9560.65.054).

difficult and intractable was the restructuring of the railroad. As with other operations, Bressler began by searching outside the organization for new leaders, paying them well and giving them their head.

The rate of turnover of chief executives is some measure of the challenge to experienced and talented executives and the demanding goals set for them. The first rail CEO under Bressler (1981) was Richard Grayson, former CEO of the Frisco, which had been merged with BN under Menk's initiative before Bressler arrived. In 1982, Grayson moved up to be vice chairman of Burlington Northern Inc., the holding company. He was succeeded as CEO of the railroad by Walter Drexel, a former finance and tax executive with Atlantic Richfield who arrived from Anaconda Copper, with whom Bressler had worked in his previous appointment. Drexel had been hired initially as BNI's senior vice president, planning. During Drexel's tenure, which extended through 1986, Darius Gaskins, a former chairman of the Interstate Commerce Commission (under President Jimmy Carter) who was commonly regarded as a probusiness commissioner, had joined BN railroad to head up the marketing function. In 1985, Gaskins became president and chief operating officer and, in 1986, chief executive officer. At the same time Drexel became vice chairman of the BN holding company. In 1988, Gaskins was succeeded by Gerald Grinstein, former CEO of Western Airlines, who had previously served on BN's board.

This turnover of leadership at the railroad was partially symptomatic of the restless search for new initiatives that would improve profitability, and of the persistent obstacles and frustrations that blunted each successive avenue of attack. Some of the major initiatives designed to make a difference, and the response from BN's several constituencies, are outlined below.

Three major events set the stage for what was about to occur at the BN railroad as the decade of the 1980s began. One was the completion of the major rebuilding of roadbed and equipment under Menk. The second was the implementation of the merger with the Frisco, which Menk had negotiated prior to retirement. The third was the enactment by Congress of the Staggers Act, in the fall of 1980, under the Carter administration. It began a gradual deregulation of the railroads with the intent of making the nation's rail system more efficient and profitable, and competitive with alternative surface transportation. Deregulation allowed for more control over rate setting, negotiation of long-term contracts, the abandonment of unprofitable lines, and a more receptive atmosphere for rail consolidation.[2] It also removed the protection the railroads had enjoyed from antitrust action for collusion on rate setting.

Bressler considered that one of his first priorities at the railroad—and elsewhere in the BN operation—was to terminate or renegotiate outstanding long-term agreements which had locked in revenues at a level totally out of line with the subsequent cost structure. Electric power utilities, which were fueled by Western coal, represented a key customer base. In aggressively pushing increases in shipments in the 1970s, BN had issued letters of agreement on rates that were interpreted as long-term contracts. Subsequently labor costs doubled and diesel fuel costs rose from 12 cents to 90 cents a gallon. Bressler personally undertook to visit all 37 of BN's utility customers to press for an economic return to the railroad, which would be in the long-term interest of all parties.[3]

In an effort to bring organizational focus to the needs of the customer, marketing was reorganized around commodity categories. The 1982 hiring of Darius Gaskins as a new BN senior vice president of marketing and sales had been a move to further heighten the importance of that aspect of the company's services. New marketing approaches and techniques included a more cooperative attitude toward the trucking industry through reload centers for break bulk shipment and backhaul and increased emphasis on intermodal facilities.[4]

Complementing the emphasis on increased revenues was a concerted drive to lower costs. At the outset of his tenure, Bressler had inherited a railroad with one of the highest operating ratios in the industry (operating costs as a percentage of operating revenues). Economies included a reduced number of mechanical facilities, yards and terminals, mechanization and computerization of manual functions, more efficient work rules, incentives for increased productivity, new investment focused on cost reduction, including more fuel efficient locomotives (BN was the largest diesel fuel consumer in the United States next to the U.S. government), and reduced inventories.

The largest single cost component was payroll. It was the most difficult to manage since 89% of the employee force worked under union contracts monitored by strong and battle-hardened unions and

[2] Roger G. Noll and Bruce M. Owen, *The Political Economy of Deregulation*, chap. 7, Regulatory Reform: What Actually Happened, Case #1. *Rail and Trucking Deregulation* (T.G. Moore) (Washington, D.C.: The American Enterprise Institute for Public Policy Research, 1983).

[3] "A Railroad for the Long Haul," *Forbes*, April 27, 1981, pp. 120–126.

[4] "BN Marketing Makes Its Mark," *Railway Age*, October 1984, pp. 32–35.

backed by federal legislation and regulation.[5] It was a long-term objective for Bressler to reduce operating crews from four-plus employees to two. It was public information that management hoped to cut the original work force it inherited from the BN-Frisco merger in half. The actual employee count was as follows:

1981	55,347	100%
1982	46,015	83%
1983	40,914	74%
1984	39,791	72%
1985	37,885	68%
1986	35,109	63%
1987	32,809	59%
1988	32,402	58%[6]

Another key component of the cost-reduction process was the program of abandonment of unprofitable feeder lines, the outer branches on the rail system. Had Bressler had his way, he would have totally defoliated the BN system, leaving only the East-West trunk line for long-haul freight, either operated by BN or leased to other users. Some feeder lines were sold to nonunion local short-line operators who continued the service at a much lower cost. Labor costs for nonunion employees could be reduced by as much as 50%.

There was a lengthy approval process when branch lines were sold to other railroads. Although the process of line abandonment was vigorously pursued, the initiative was blunted by political opposition at the local and national levels. Inevitably, the plan for branch line reduction, even in its early stages, was vigorously opposed by local shippers, the local communities and their political representatives, and the unions. It soon became a political hot potato. The ICC slowed the process of approval, and in 1981 Senator Mark Andrews of North Dakota succeeded in a budget amendment that shut off funds for processing abandonment proposals.

However, the effort bore some results. Bressler had originally targeted a reduction of 8,000 miles (28%). By 1987, BN had since 1980 managed to reduce its rail system by 4,400 miles.

Competition with other railroads and with nonrail bulk carriers had been for BN a perennial problem, which intensified with the onset of deregulation. Among the railroads, one stood out as

[5] *Forbes*, November 16, 1987, p. 86.
[6] *Moody's Transportation Manual*, 1988, p. 13.

the pacesetter for BN and its management: Union Pacific, another resource-rich railroad. During the 1970s, Union Pacific's return to shareholders had been a compound annual rate of 18%, double that of BN. For Bressler the competitive challenge was heightened by the fact that William Cook, CEO of Union Pacific, had been a contemporary of his at General Electric, where Bressler had landed fresh out of the Tuck Business School.

A critical area of potential competition was the transportation of coal from the Powder River Basin on which BN had a historical monopoly. Potential competition would be from other railroads and a possible coal slurry pipeline, which never materialized. The specific rail threat came from the Chicago and Northwestern Railroad, which had been endeavoring to find its way into some of the Powder River Basin coal traffic, with BN's help or without. In 1981, the ICC authorized the C & NW to build a key 56-mile connection line with the Union Pacific system, thus setting in place a subsequent ICC-imposed joint ownership with BN of trackage to the Powder River Basin. C & NW was a financially weak railroad, but with Union Pacific backing it arranged the financing of the half-billion-dollar investment required to upgrade these facilities.

The results became apparent in 1985, by which time C & NW's access route had been completed. By 1986, BN's revenues from coal had declined by $579 million, 31% of their 1984 volume. In the process, C & NW's competition offset most of the cost savings that BN had fought so hard to produce.

Despite these periodic setbacks to management's drive to upgrade railroad performance, steady improvement in efficiency was made during the 1980s. The data shown in Table 7.1 provide some objective evidence of slow but steady progress.

This improvement in efficiency was reflected in steady improvement in rail "cash flow" (net income, after-tax, plus noncash charges) through 1985, after which revenues declined, owing primarily to reduced volume and lower prices on coal shipments:

	Gross "Cash Flow" (thousands)
1981	$370,533
1982	377,530
1983	627,945
1984	777,159
1985	723,921
1986	393,362
1987	642,340

Table 7.1   Burlington Northern Freight Train Performance

Year	Tonnage Originated (millions of tons)	Average Haul Miles (miles)	Train Miles per Train Hour (miles)	Net /Tons per Car (tons)	Operating Ratio[a] (%)
1979	164	641	20.7	68.6	95.5
1980	184	650	22.6	72.5	92.2
1981	205	681	23.0	68.3	92.1
1982	197	689	23.2	70.0	93.7
1983	213	718	22.8	71.4	82.2
1984	240	751	22.5	72.9	78.6
1985	220	7,53	22.7	72.2	80.7
1986	220	7,57	23.8	71.5	97.3
1987	238	770	24.4	73.9	85.1
1988	261	761	24.1	74.9	85.3

[a] Operating costs as a percentage of operating revenues.
Source: Moody's Transportation Manual, 1988, pp. 11–14.

As a result, substantial sums were dividended up to the holding company for investment in resources and distribution to shareholders. In the 1983–1987 period, the railroad paid out cash dividends totaling $1.926 billion.[7] It is interesting to note that this was roughly equal to the capital expended in the preceding decade by Lou Menk for a major upgrade of roadbed and equipment. This cash drain was of serious concern to the primary rail constituencies, just as the cash drain from resources to the railroad had been a concern of the resources management and its constituencies in the prior decade.[8]

Options Considered

While Bressler's central long-term strategy for the release of BN's full economic potential continued to evolve, once in a while diversions occurred which had the potential to influence the course of events. One of these was the threat of takeover, rumblings of which surfaced in the press from time to time. In early 1987, T. Boone Pickens was rumored to be interested in BN, undoubtedly attracted by BN's oil and gas interests. At year-end 1986, Pickens's Mesa Lim-

[7] Ibid.
[8] "Burlington Northern's Cash Cow," *Business Week*, March 8, 1982, pp. 113–114.

ited Partnership was reported as owning 1.8 million shares of BN stock (2.5%).[9]

In an August 1987 *Business Week* article titled "Will a Takeover Derail Burlington Northern's Makeover?" Bressler was quoted, as he had been on a number of other occasions, to the effect that he would gladly recommend sale of the company "at the right price."[10] He was known to believe that the intractable problems of the railroad were BN's real poison-pill defense against unwanted raiders. The threat from Pickens never materialized, but BN had been sufficiently concerned to pass its own formal poison-pill defense in July 1986 over some board resistance. As is generally recognized by incumbent managements, such defenses are no lasting protection against a determined acquirer but do serve to slow down the process and perhaps improve the negotiated terms.

At about the same time, a Wall Street firm had brought forward the idea of a management buyout. Bressler brought the idea to the top management who would be involved if such a plan was to be implemented. As is customary in such plans, a heavy debt burden would be substituted for most of the outstanding equity. While some of the top managers liked the idea, it was opposed by others, and the suggestion was quickly rejected.

The concept of increased leverage as a component of value enhancement was not, however, totally rejected. From 1982 to 1986, the debt-equity ratio had been rising, from .49 to 1.04. In October 1987, BN announced a plan to buy back 5 million shares, 7% of its outstanding common stock. However, the plan was never fully implemented.

In the end these various initiatives did not have a material effect on the main course of events, which related to the fundamental economic viability of the railroad and the resource enterprises. It was here that the ultimate success or failure of BN's restructuring would be played out.

The Crowning Blow

At the core of cost containment on the railroad was the employee payroll. Between 1981 and 1987 the number of employees

[9] *Houston Chronicle*, February 22, 1987, p. 5.
[10] *Business Week*, August 3, 1987, pp. 66–67.

decreased by 40%. During the same period, average compensation per employee increased by 43%. As a result, in spite of a major reduction in the employee count, the absolute dollars of total payroll increased over this period—discouraging to a management committed to doubling return on equity.

The heart of the problem of further reduction was seen to be the size of the operating crews. It was in anticipation of a major showdown with the unions on this issue that the two-track restructuring strategy was based—build the economic potential of the resources enterprises as a lever to pry loose major cost reductions on the railroad system. However, the work-crew problem stubbornly refused to budge.

In an effort to appeal directly to the workers, BN had instituted economic education seminars, and workers were paid $100 to attend a four-hour meeting. Two-thirds of the work force attended. They were told that BN had averaged a 7% return on invested capital between 1982 and 1986, versus 14% by leading trucking companies. They were told that BN needed a return between 8 and 14% to grow and attract new capital. There was no detectable response from the unionized work force.

BN had made no secret of its determination to gain work-crew concessions and its intention to go it alone if necessary, breaking with the railroad tradition of negotiating as an industry. The key to independent action was the ability of a single railroad to take a strike without involving the other railroads, which would precipitate a national emergency and congressional intervention. These plans were ultimately thwarted by a strike action outside the BN system— against the Maine Central Railroad and its parent company, Guilford Industries, a New England transportation holding company. As part of this action, the unions picketed—and were sued by—interchanging railroads. The legal process ultimately reached the Supreme Court, which ruled in April 1987 that secondary boycotts by striking unions were legal. This effectively ended BN's hope of successful independent action.

Frustrated by union opposition to crew reduction, but relentlessly innovative, BN had been developing a novel approach to work-crew reduction on its main line between Minneapolis and Seattle. The plan became public knowledge in 1987. A new subsidiary company would be formed. Called Winona Bridge, it would lease the main line from BN and hire nonunion workers to operate the trains. Initially, the courts issued a restraining order against a union strike threat over the plan, and the ICC approved the lease in November 1987. However, as the legal wrangling progressed, amid plans by BN to reduce crew size to two operators on each train, it became clear that the plan was in trouble. In June 1988, the Eighth Circuit Court of Appeals upheld a lower court's ruling against the proposed work-rule changes on the Winona line and the lower court's refusal to grant a strike injunction. In October the plan was dropped by BN.

The End of an Era

The action of the Supreme Court in confirming the right of unions to implement secondary boycotts effectively put an end to Bressler's initial long-term restructuring strategy for the BN railroad. As the end of Bressler's self-imposed decade of tenure approached, he elected to play his remaining card: the complete separation of ownership of the resources enterprises from that of the railroad. On June 2, 1988, BN announced its intention to sell 13% of the stock of Burlington Resources Inc., a newly created subsidiary which held the parent's timber, real estate, coal, oil, and gas properties. The purpose was to establish a market value for the stock in anticipation of a tax-free distribution of the remainder of the stock as a dividend to the shareholders of BNI, which would then continue to exist solely as a railroad enterprise. After the spin-off, former shareholders of the holding company would hold shares in the two separate companies, each of which would operate and trade independently of the other. The initial offering sold on July 7 at $25.50 per share (implicit market value of the new resources company: $3.9 billion).

The first market response to the announcement of the spin-off is a measure of the support that BN shareholders gave to the decisions of corporate leadership. The spin-off was announced before the market opened on June 2, 1988. Adjusting for changes in the market as a whole, BN common rose from the close of trading on June 1 to the close of trading on June 2 by 3.12%. It was clearly a welcome move.

On October 20, 1988, BNI announced that its board had approved the spin-off of the resources company to shareholders of record on December 18 and that new chief executive officers had been elected to each company. "Following the distribution, BNI's principal operation will be Burlington Northern Railroad."[11] Immediately prior

---

[11] Company release.

to this announcement, the resources stock had traded at $31.75 per share.

The primary intent of the spin-off was obvious. It was to free up the potential equity value of the resource enterprises from the persistent drag of inferior rail earnings performance which, despite hard-earned improvement, was still below competitive equity returns. As separate entities, each was expected to reach its own true market value. Beyond this, however, there was an important secondary effect, which a railroad bond analyst, Isabel Benham, was quick to note.

The ultimate goal of industry today is to enhance shareholders' value. In the rail area, this is being accomplished through the unwinding of railroad-based conglomerates, leverage buyouts, rail mergers, rail stock repurchase programs, one-time large dividend payments, spin-offs of non-rail assets from the rail conglomerate.

In implementing these programs, the rails have become highly leveraged companies with the added risk inherent in a high level of debt exposure. Also, in the process, little consideration has been given to the rail bondholder. In fact, in several instances, the financial success of a program has been at the expense of the bondholder. One rail restructuring resulted in a multi-billion dollar gain for the Company's equity holders, all of which was made possible only because the bondholders gave to the corporate entity, for a mere pittance, the very assets under their mortgage lien which made the equity gain possible . . .

The following table shows the ratios of debt to total capitalization of those rails which recently have undertaken the enhancement of shareholders' value through restructuring programs:

Class I Railroads
Debt-Equity Position
12/31/88
-millions-

Restructured Rails	Long-Term Debt	Com. Equity	Debt % of Total Capital
Burlington Northern	$2,723	$ 918	75%
Sante Fe	3,405	483	88%
CSX	3,032	3,392	47%
Union Pacific	3,332	4,402	43%

Benham goes on to comment specifically on BNI.

With the release of the land and mineral rights, BN management decided to create a new subsidiary, Burlington Resources Inc. (BR), to hold all of the Company's natural resource assets. Significantly, none of the debt, a large part of which was issued to finance or develop the properties of the new Resources Company, was transferred or assumed by the new subsidiary. Rather the debt was left with the parent holding company whose only remaining asset was the railroad. In short, rail earnings were expected to take care of all rail as well as outstanding non-rail debt . . .

Before the restructuring process, the total market value of BNI common shares was about $4.5 billion (May 19, 1988). The post-restructuring market value (January 20, 1989) was about $7.5 billion with shares of Burlington Resources selling at 38¾ and the railroad shares at 23¼. In short, the original BNI shareholders had an enhancement of their investment value of $3 billion in less than one year. Contrast this with the $35 million paid bondholders for the release of their assets from under the Northern Pacific bonds.

Today, $117 million par value of the Northern Pacific bonds remain outstanding and are only a small part of BNI's total debt obligations of $2.6 billion, all of which must be serviced by the railroad. On a pro forma basis, pretax coverage of interest was 2.2x as of September 30, 1988 as compared with 5.6x as of December 31, 1987, the year before the restructuring program. Also, the debt-to-equity ratio which was 41% at the 1987 year-end, was 72% as of September 30, 1988.

She concludes with the following query:

With the debt side of the balance sheet so overloaded and bondholders' interests so neglected in current restructuring programs, where will the capital come from to finance the future capital needs of the industry? In the next decade, the industry capital needs are expected to reach $7–$8 billion annually. Only through such expenditures can the industry grow and continue to serve the public interest. But will long-term investors forget the rape of their rail bonds in the 1980 decade and provide the necessary capital in the mid-1990s? If not, and if rail equities continue to run a collision course with rail debt, the future viability of the industry may be seriously threatened. The situation is even more threatening when it is realized that the rails, unlike other industries, are operated in the public interest which requires a strong and viable transportation network.[12]

In response to this report, Richard Bressler sent Benham the following letter, with copies to his board:

[12] Isabel H. Benham, "The Forgotten Bondholder and the Impact on Rail Capital Programs," Princeton: Kane Research Inc., May 11, 1989.

Dear Isabel:

I appreciate receiving a copy of your report entitled "The Forgotten Rail Bondholder." I have no problem with the facts as you recite them in the BN case, but I think your interpretation is way off the mark. Let me give you my reasoning.

The effort to obtain release from the NP mortgages started many years before the idea to split the company into two parts. We simply foresaw the day when the proceeds from the Lands would far exceed the amounts necessary to be reinvested in the old NP Railroad. That the release of the mortgages permitted the split of the company was a matter of fortuitous timing. However, to say that the bondholders got a pittance compared to the increase in value to the equity owners overlooks the nature of the contract between the bondholders and the company. As you correctly point out we first attempted to defease the bonds with US Government securities which would have immeasurably improved the bondholders' security but they blocked that and chose to use their nuisance value to bargain for compensation. They accepted the deal and for you to say that they have been somehow ill-treated does not square with reality. As you probably know these bonds were held by institutions or sophisticated investors who look after their interests very well.

The principal reason for the split of the Company was our lack of success in convincing the market [the transportation analysts community] of the substantial asset values that were not reflected in the BN stock price. Nothing much happened to the stock until we were able to attract more knowledgeable analysts after the announcement of the initial offering of the Resource stock. You may recall that the settlement with the bondholders preceded the Resource announcement by several months and the stock continued to be followed largely by the transportation analysts. At the time of the offering such well known analysts as Grahme Lidgerwood and Joel Price opined that the expected offering price of $25–$28 was too high. I found it interesting that when First Boston assigned their energy analyst to BR stock he immediately said it was worth in the 40s. So if one wants to be kind about why the stock soared after the split you can say it was the imperfection of the marketplace.

Now to your other point about the leverage at the railroad, I agree that it is too high and it was not planned that way. Because the railroad had thrown off excess cash in recent years, the restructuring was designed to essentially take two years excess cash flow in advance and give it to Resources. That amount of additional debt we were comfortable with in any viable scenario; however, the amount of the ETSI settlement took us by surprise. As you know that $175 million settlement occurred at the end of 1988 and by that time there was already a minority interest in Resources which effectively shut the door on any reshuffling of the debt load. Reduction of debt is now the number one priority at BNI and I am confident it will be accomplished.

To your final thought as to whether or not there will be sufficient capital available to meet the future requirements of the industry, I was surprised that you did not mention the problem of sub-par profitability of the industry. If the BN or any other railroad can achieve the profitability it should have, I have no fears about obtaining the required capital.

This intriguing dialogue between the chief executive of BNI and the investment community gets to the heart of the issues of restructuring in the 1980s: Who should be the ultimate beneficiary of corporate financial management?

One further point should be made. Though Bressler states that the resultant excessive leverage of the railroad "was not planned that way," it had a major consequence for the railroad restructuring. It is widely recognized that an intentional consequence of the excessive leveraging of many restructurings in the 1980s, with its attendant heavy demands for debt servicing, was to force a strict cash-flow discipline on the organization's cost and revenue structure. The original BNI loans and credit rating were generously backed by asset values, albeit much of them undeveloped. With these gone, BNI debt security was based primarily on the operating funds flows of the railroad. This fact imposed a new discipline on both railroad management *and* labor, which neither they nor their customers or host communities could long ignore. There is no doubt that Bressler was well aware of this consequence. The restructuring of the railroad would continue after Bressler's retirement under the objective and dispassionate eye of the major bondholders.

The Bottom Line

To a long-term equity investor, the specific means by which management chooses to advance the interests of an enterprise are secondary to the lasting consequences for shareholder wealth. Of course, the yardstick of performance is necessarily relative, not absolute, and must be measured against the performance of alternative investment of comparable risk. Thus, in evaluating the success of the Bressler era of voluntary restructuring at BNI during the 1980s, one must consider two standards of comparison: the performance of the equity under his predecessor at BNI during the 1970s and the performance of other comparable equity investments during the 1980s.

Management cannot be held accountable for the broad move-

ments of the equity market as a whole—the environmental tides that
raise or lower all boats. Management must focus on those elements
of corporate investment and return on investment over which it exer-
cises a degree of control. The most commonly used internal standard
in this respect is (book) return on (book) equity. In addition, I use
two other standards that reflect the capital-market response to this
performance:

- The market-to-book ratio: the market value per share of common
  equity divided by the book value per share
- The total equity return: the combination of the annual gain or
  loss in market value of the stock plus the cash dividends paid.
  This is the measure of the total financial benefit (as a percentage
  of market value) received by the shareholder as a result of owning
  a share of BNI stock for a year, or as an average return over
  several years.

We begin by looking at return on equity (net income after taxes,
and before extraordinary charges, on book equity) as seen in Figure
7.1. The figure tracks Burlington Northern's consolidated ROE per-

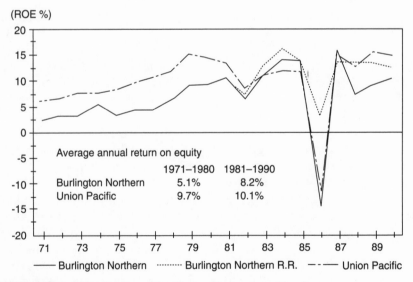

Figure 7.1   Burlington Northern Return on Equity
(vs. Union Pacific)

Source: Standard & Poor's COMPUSTAT.

formance throughout the period and compares it with its "competitor of choice," Union Pacific. It also shows BN rail as a separate ROE since 1981, the period when Bressler moved aggressively to improve the performance of the resources component.

The most impressive single statistic of this competitive performance lies in the decade averages. In the 1970s, BN had an average ROE of 5.1% (Treasury bills averaged around 6%) whereas Union Pacific's ROE was 9.7%. In the 1980s, BN's average ROE increased to 8.2%. By comparison, Union Pacific's remained almost constant (10.1%). It was an impressive turnaround, though not a return with which either Bressler or his shareholders were satisfied. During the 1980s, riskless Treasury bills had increased their average return to about 9%.

As has been noted, Lou Menk had been deeply disappointed by the financial performance of the 1970s. Predictably, returns had been adversely affected by a program of heavy investment, but the promised rewards of coal development never materialized during his tenure. In some degree it was Bressler who, in the 1980s, reaped the benefits of that investment. There is, however, no denying the improvement brought by the restructuring process of the 1980s, slow and painful as it was.

The response of equity holders to these results is reflected in Figure 7.2, which shows the market-value to book-value ratio for BN, the railroad industry,[13] and the Standard & Poor's 500 index of industrial common stocks. The first thing to note is the remarkably persistent decline in the market-to-book ratio as a whole (the S&P 500 index) from 1972 to 1981 (market price 3.89 times book in 1972, 1.44 times book in 1981). The trend then reversed in the 1980s and by 1989 was up to 2.94 times book. Through the 1970s the market as a whole was increasingly discounting the effect of improvements in reported earnings achieved by corporate management.

However, this was not true of the railroad industry or of Burlington Northern. In 1970, the market-to-book multipliers were extremely depressed: .58 times book for the industry and .25 times book for BN. These gradually improved over the decade, and by 1980 both the industry and BN had risen to approximate equality of market and book values. The general trend continued upward in the 1980s, reaching a peak in 1988 for the industry of 3.13 times book and

[13] The industry index was constructed from the performance of five companies: CSX, Canadian Pacific, Norfolk and Southern, Santa Fe, and Union Pacific.

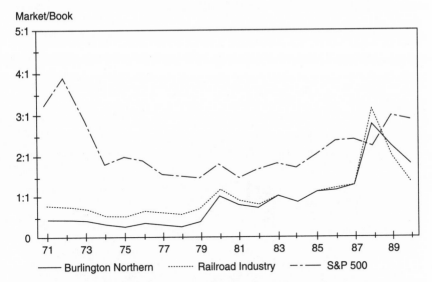

Figure 7.2   Burlington Northern vs. Railroad Industry
(Market-to-Book Ratio)

Source: Standard & Poor's COMPUSTAT.

for BN of 2.74 times book value. These ratios record the secular improvement in the market's valuation of railroad performance over the two decades, in which BN shared.

Finally, and most important, Figure 7.3 shows the percentage of total equity returns over the two decades, reflecting the combined benefit of capital gains and dividends paid—the true equity payoff. We compare the Bressler performance pre- and post-spin-off of the resources industries with the performance under Menk in the 1970s. As with all such statistics, it is important to note that the absolute performance over any period is strongly influenced by the dates chosen for beginning and ending of the era in question and the general market conditions at that time. So, in part, the record is influenced by the arbitrary timing of the interval. However, there is no denying that the *relative* performance against other companies is strong evidence of the effectiveness of a particular managerial performance.

Figure 7.3 is a remarkable testimony to the results of the voluntary restructuring under Bressler. Not only were the average equity returns virtually doubled from 10.63% to 20.74% before the spin-off and tripled to 29.59% thereafter, but the relative performance com-

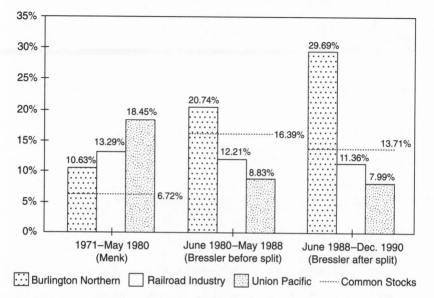

Figure 7.3   Burlington Northern Total Equity Return (Average Annual Return)

Source: © *Stocks, Bonds, Bills, and Inflation 1993 Yearbook*^{TM}, Ibbotson Associates, Chicago (annually updates work by Roger G. Ibbotson and Rex A. Sinquefield). Used with permission. All rights reserved.

pared with Union Pacific and the industry was conclusively reversed. Further, though the time frame was necessarily short, the benefits from the spin-off of resources are quite clear. The evidence of shareholder benefit speaks for itself. What remains unclear, since the data are not available, is the extent to which these gains represented a sacrifice by other corporate constituencies as opposed to new value-added—surely, some of each.

Postscript

Subsequent to the date of the BN case, the following events are worthy of note. On January 1, 1989, Richard Bressler resigned as chief executive officer of BNI and Burlington Resources, remaining as chairman of the board until October 1990. In June 1989, the assets of Plum Creek Timber were sold to a master limited partnership with units offered to the investing public. Bressler served as chairman of that partnership until December 1992. On December 13, 1990, Burlington Resources announced its intention to effect a tax-free separation of El Paso Natural Gas, which was accomplished in 1992. Bressler serves as chairman of El Paso. As of April 30, 1993, the market value of the four publicly held companies aggregated $13.3 billion. The market value of Burlington Northern during 1980 was less than $1 billion.

CHAPTER 8

Stimulus to Change:
CPC International, Inc.

Chapter Overview

In the summer of 1986, press comment and rumors abounded in the financial community that CPC International was ripe for major restructuring. For decades CPC's business had two principal components: corn wet-milling, a commodity business producing starches, oils, and sweeteners, and packaged proprietary grocery products with such well-known brand names as Hellman's mayonnaise and Skippy peanut butter. Further, it was heavily international in production and sales. For years analysts had complained about the uneven performance of the two segments and questioned the wisdom of the persistent flow of internally generated funds from the more profitable, cash-surplus grocery products to less profitable commodity investments.

At a *Wall Street Transcript* round table on foods stocks in August 1986, Ronald L. Strauss, analyst with William Blair and Company, expressed the sentiments of the panel when he said:

The biggest potential in CPC is if its management will decide one day to restructure this company. I realize that many investors are very skeptical about it . . . The only thing I can say is, when I look at the structure of the company, this is definitely a company in need of restructuring, that can dramatically benefit from [it], and enhance shareholders' value. The stock's multiple is clearly being depressed . . . It just makes so much sense that I find it hard to believe that eventually management will not come to the same conclusion.[1]

Two months later, in an article headed "CPC International Attracts Sudden Attention as Stock Price Rises amid Takeover Rumors," *The Wall Street Journal*'s column "Heard on the Street" reported:

Long-neglected CPC International is suddenly getting attention.

Until recently, CPC seemed untouched by the storms sweeping the food industry over the past year. It sat on the sidelines while several brand-name food companies were swallowed up or took defensive measures to boost their stock price.

But now CPC is being drawn into the maelstrom. Over the past week, CPC shares have spurted about 10 points on unusually large volumes, handled mainly by Drexel, Burnham, Lambert and Morgan Stanley, traders say. There are rumors that Con Agra, Revlon or CPC management may bid for the company. Foreign consumer companies and U.S. tobacco concerns are also cited as possible buyers.[2]

On October 31, *The Wall Street Journal* reported that Ronald O. Perelman, a prominent activist in the market for corporate control who had launched a successful takeover of Revlon, was the individual whose recent acquisitions of CPC shares had stimulated the run-up in their price. A trader was quoted: "People think he's very serious." The rumor was true, as later events revealed.

This action by Perelman triggered an immediate all-out response from CPC management in defense of independence and self-determination. Over the subsequent weeks and months, a radical restructuring occurred which, in part at least, was the response for which analysts had been hoping. Independence was preserved, but only by a dramatic acceleration of the pace of change. At its annual meeting in April 1987, CPC's chief executive, James Eiszner, stated that the results of the takeover attempt "were not a change in plans, but an acceleration of plans." There was much truth in this statement, but the "acceleration of plans" was much like that which a mountain-climbing team experiences when suddenly confronted by an avalanche breaking loose above it.

---

[1] *The Wall Street Transcript*, August 4, 1986, p. 82725.
[2] *The Wall Street Journal*, October 14, 1986, p. 67.

The Origins of the Pre-1986 Structure

CPC began its corporate existence in 1906 as the Corn Products Refining Company engaged in the manufacture of corn wet-milling products—corn starch, syrup, and oil. They were produced in the United States and sold in bulk in the United States and Europe. Today corn wet-milling products are used in 60 different industries, among them paper, baking, canning, confection, textiles, chemicals, and pharmaceuticals. A major development in recent years has been the production of high-fructose corn syrup as a sweetener for soft drinks.

Its early years were characterized by slow, uncertain progress. Antitrust action in the early 1900s served to restrict growth in the United States and drove the company to diversify its overseas operations. However, the results were modest at best. Between 1917 and 1945, sales had risen from $100 million to $106 million and profits had declined from $11 million to under $9 million.[3] In 1956 a new chief executive, William T. Brady, became the catalyst of change and the mastermind of Corn Products' first major restructuring. In a move designed to diversify the product line and increase profitability and growth of the company, Brady acquired a controlling interest in the German-based manufacturer of dehydrated soups, C.H. Knorr Company. In the same year (1958) he negotiated a major merger with the Best Foods Company (U.S.). Dropping the original emphasis on industrial refining, the company became Corn Products Company. Best Foods was a successful packaged, branded grocery products company operating nationally. Though still dominated by the corn wet-milling division at the time of the merger, CPC had embarked on a path that would see the consumer foods divisions equal and then surpass corn wet-milling in gross revenues and particularly in profits by the 1970s.

Brady, who retired as CEO in 1963, was followed in rapid succession by two men who left no lasting mark on the company. In 1968, Howard Harder, at the age of 52, became the third chief executive to follow Brady. Harder had spent his entire business career at Corn Products, beginning as an office boy in 1937, and reached corporate leadership through managerial positions in finance. By 1967, sales had risen to $1.1 billion, but profits had for several years been flat at around $50 million.

---

[3] *Forbes*, October 15, 1968, p. 59.

It is not surprising that a finance-trained CEO would see his competitive challenge through the lens of the capital markets. At the time of his appointment he announced that his number one goal was to make earnings-per-share growth "at least equal to the companies with whom I'm competing for capital."[4] The statement also reveals the outdated metric of performance in which growth was perceived to be the key to higher price-earnings ratios, though the specific linkage was never clearly articulated. In an effort to escape the problems of mature product lines, Harder launched a new strategy of unrelated diversification: bulk pharmaceuticals and chemicals, aerosol packaging, industrial catering and restaurants, and manpower training and education. It was in keeping with the conventional wisdom of the time. To reflect the diversified, worldwide image, the name of the company was changed to CPC International.

His term was short, and when Harder retired "for personal reasons" in 1972, the record of achievement was modest. Though sales had grown, from $1 billion to $1.5 billion, net income had remained flat: $51 million in 1967, $52 million in 1972. The proportion between industrial and consumer products continued to shift, and by 1972 it was 40% industrial, 50% consumer, and 10% other. The new diversification had virtually no impact on overall performance. The strategy never had solid management support. In retrospect, the only acquisition of lasting importance (1970) was S.B. Thomas (English muffins), which was to become the nucleus of a significant bakery products segment. It proved to be a very profitable investment.

In 1972, James W. McKee, Jr., age 49, became the fourth chief executive of CPC in ten years. The burnout rate of leadership had become an obvious problem and McKee was the solution. For its new CEO, CPC turned once again to a man who had spent his entire working career with the company, again in finance. The new twist, in keeping with the fact that corporate sales were then 55% outside the United States, was that McKee's experience was primarily in overseas operations. When he first joined the company he was almost immediately posted abroad in finance functions, first in Italy, then Brazil (and Cuba), where he became general manager, and he remained abroad from 1947 to 1964, when he returned to corporate headquarters as controller. He became vice president, finance in 1965 and president and COO in 1969. Becoming CEO in 1972, McKee remained at the helm of CPC until 1984 and, by his own criteria,

[4]Ibid.

achieved a remarkable record of success. The issue we will face later is: Were those the right criteria?

CPC under McKee

During the McKee era at CPC the company adopted the motto Do Better What You Do Best. In a speech before a CPC management conference in 1974, McKee, commenting on the 15 years since the merger with Best Foods, said:

Although other market and economic factors have also been at work, it is difficult not to conclude that, based on the way our international businesses were progressing, we do much better when we concentrate on what we know best than what we have been able to do when we venture too far afield.

More than that, however, it also seems to indicate that we did not invest sufficiently in our basic businesses in the U.S. because on closer examination one of the major factors in the lack of total growth has been because we were not even maintaining the profitability on one major segment of our total business—the corn wet-milling or industrial business in the U.S.

This became the one area which, if successfully turned around, could make the single most significant contribution to our earnings results . . . But this is still a long-term program.[5]

A slight paraphrase of the corporate motto would be Do Better What You *Know* Best, and what McKee knew best, judging by his on-the-job experience, was the industrial corn wet-milling business, particularly in its global setting. This dedication to the restoration of the industrial corn wet-milling business as a strong competitive and profitable enterprise was the unique feature of the McKee era.

As with all corporate leaders, McKee had a number of defining personal attributes, as viewed by his long-term colleagues. These included intense loyalty to the organization and to individuals, strong convictions (some would say he was "stubborn"), a propensity to act deliberately and only after thorough analysis and discussion, and a commitment to financial conservatism. He saw issues and strategic decisions in a long-term perspective, with the survival and well-being of the corporate enterprise paramount.

His first move on becoming CEO was to undo the unrelated diversification initiated by his predecessor, Harder. He regarded

---

[5] Unpublished internal document.

Table 8.1 CPC Financial Performance Analysis

			1974	1973	1972	1971	1970
Return on Sales ×	=	Earnings Sales	3.49%	4.03%	4.15%	3.67%	4.50%
Asset Turnover =	=	Sales Assets	2.15×	1.74×	1.50×	1.43×	1.44×
Return on Assets ×	=	Earnings Assets	7.5%	7.0%	6.2%	5.3%	6.5%
Leverage =	=	Assets Equity	2.10×	2.05×	2.13×	2.17×	2.10×
Return on Shareholders' Equity	=	Earnings Equity	15.8%	14.3%	13.2%	11.5%	13.6%

Note: Earnings are before extraordinary items.

those as unproductive and distracting from the primary task of strengthening the core industries. The discontinued, sold, or spun off businesses were chemicals and pharmaceuticals, seeds, cake frosting, agribusiness operations, restaurants, and infant formulas. "The bases of our company," he said, "are its consumer and industrial businesses (—world-wide)." There was some management opposition to this action, based on the principle of honoring past commitments; "abrogating treaties" was considered by some as a dishonorable breach of trust.

One measure of management's attitude to its shareholders is the information on financial performance it considers important and is willing to share with them. Apart from mandatory financial statements, it is typical that other published data come and go over the years, depending on how well or poorly they serve the positive image of accomplishment. A significant artifact of the McKee era was a table which, for the first time, focused on the *quality* of earnings through rate of return data (see Table 8.1).[6]

The table draws the reader's attention to the translation of return on sales into a return on equity via the "balance sheet multipliers," turnover of assets, and debt leverage. It implicitly accepts management accountability for a competitive and, hopefully, improving ROE—return per dollar of shareholders' invested capital. The re-

[6]CPC International, *Annual Report*, 1974.

markable thing about this table is that it was continued without interruption during McKee's entire career—and continues to this day. Later in this chapter, Figure 8.1 illustrates this performance through the two decades of the 1970s and 1980s.

For many years before McKee's accession to power at CPC, management had debated the wisdom of new investment in corn wet-milling. The diversification into branded grocery products was the most visible result of that debate, and the continuing shift in the balance of corporate sales and profits toward the proprietary product lines was further evidence. At the same time, however, there was an unwavering dedication to preserve a position of leadership in the basic commodity market, which led inescapably to the confrontation with the capital-market mentality of the 1980s.

In the area of corn wet-milling, the most critical decision for McKee was what to do with the company's North American production facilities, which were becoming outdated just when CPC was experiencing increasing pressure from major competitors. It was inherently a capital-intensive, high-volume, low-margin industry subject to supply and demand cycles and periodic bouts of competitive overbuilding of capacity. The consequences are reflected in the data shown below, which compare CPC's return on assets between consumer foods (grocery products) and corn refining during the years 1977 to 1988.[7] Return on assets for corn wet-milling was eroding in the late 1970s and early 1980s, falling to a low point of 2.8% in 1985. CPC was continuously losing market share to old and new competitors.

CPC Return on Assets

	1988	1987	1986	1985	1984	1983	1982	1981	1980	1979	1978	1977
Return on Assets												
Consumer foods	20.8%	19.1%	19.3%	23.0%	24.6%	25.5%	31.0%	29.6%	26.8%	23.5%	23.8%	24.4%
Corn refining	11.5	9.0	4.7	2.8	6.3	6.6	10.9	12.0	8.8	11.3	10.5	12.6

CPC's response to this competitive pressure was a large new investment in plant facilities for corn wet-milling that inevitably had the immediate effect of depressing return on assets further. Between 1977 and 1982, CPC invested over $1 billion in new facilities and productivity improvement, primarily in corn wet-milling in North America.

[7] "CPC International: The Shift from Corn Refining to Consumer Foods," #N9-590-064. Boston: Harvard Business School, 1989, p. 11.

Then, in 1984, as McKee was handing off the office of chief executive officer to James Eiszner (McKee remained as chairman through 1987), he launched a new Investment for Growth program that promised a further investment of $1.5 billion, again primarily in corn wet-milling facilities. In announcing this program CPC said:

> Our proudest achievement in 1984 was that, despite the extensive demands on our day-to-day business, we put in place programs and actions which should provide the basis for a solid earnings expansion in the years ahead. Plants are being rebuilt and made more efficient, grocery product franchises strengthened and expanded, and a new and more focused management structure installed.

It was an investment designed to perpetuate McKee's unswerving commitment to the corn wet-milling industry beyond his tenure in office.

This was not, however, without vigorous internal debate by those who saw the plan diverting resources from high-return to low-return investment, particularly those who identified themselves with the grocery products enterprises. Operating cash flow (operating profit plus depreciation) from grocery products was on average four times its related new capital investment during 1979 to 1985, whereas the same ratio for corn wet-milling was barely one-to-one.[8] It was not surprising, therefore, that some were heard to complain: "Why is all our cash being spent on corn wet-milling?" Despite the opposition, McKee's stature within the company and his persuasiveness carried the day. He had the reputation of hearing out dissenters but, in the end, doing things his own way.

Judged by his own criteria, James McKee could look back to a remarkably successful accomplishment. These goals were summarized in the 1982 *Annual Report* under the heading "Well-Positioned for Growth": "Over the past decade, one of the Company's primary objectives has been to achieve steady annual real growth in sales and earnings. In striving to accomplish this objective, we have sought simultaneously to maintain a strong financial position, to optimize business opportunities, and to provide an equitable return to stockholders."

At his retirement, McKee could take justifiable pride in 44 successive quarters of increased earnings per share. On an absolute scale of growth in quantity of sales and earnings, this was a remarkable achievement. But what about the *quality* of earnings (return per dollar

[8]Company annual reports.

of investment)? The record is shown in Table 8.2. These are the previously mentioned rate of return figures regularly published by the company. From 1972 to 1982, there was persistent improvement in both return on sales and return on equity, the latter reaching a peak of 18.8% in 1980.

However, just as McKee was retiring as CEO, a window of vulnerability became apparent. There were two principal elements. One was the aforementioned continuing drag on corporate returns inherent in the corn wet-milling operation. From 1977 to 1982, the corn wet-milling ROA ranged from one-half that of consumer foods in 1977 to one-third in 1982. This negative trend had been masked in total corporate performance by a buoyant consumer foods sector.

Table 8.2   CPC Financial Performance Analysis

	Return on Sales	×	Balance Sheet Multiplier[a]	=	Return on Equity
	%		(times)		(%)
Harder					
1970	4.50		3.02		13.6
1971	3.67		3.10		11.5
McKee					
1972	4.15		3.19		13.2
1973	4.03		3.57		14.3
1974	3.49		4.51		15.8
1975	3.98		4.38		17.4
1976	4.53		3.91		17.7
1977	4.63		3.78		17.5
1978	4.57		3.83		17.6
1979	4.60		3.96		18.2
1980	4.80		3.92		18.8
1981	5.03		3.70		18.6
1982	5.66		3.28		18.5
1983[b]	3.40		3.07		10.4 [c]
1984	4.42		3.32		14.7
Eiszner					
85[b]	3.37		3.12		10.5

[a]Balance sheet multiplier is the multiple of the asset-turnover ratio times the asset-to-equity ratio.

[b]Earnings include special write-offs.

[c]Window of vulnerability.

Sources: Company annual reports.

Note: The years 1983 and 1985 include the effects of special charges and write-offs.

In 1983, this cover disappeared as overall rates of return took a sharp drop for three successive years, as seen in Table 8.2. Operating income, including consumer foods, flattened and began a gradual decline, principally owing to weak economies and currencies abroad. At this point the company, at the insistence of its financial management, chose to acknowledge the downside of its new Investment for Growth program in corn wet-milling production facilities. Residual book values in older U.S. and European plants that were to be dismantled and replaced with state-of-the-art automated facilities were written off in the amounts of $109 million in 1983 and $71 million in 1985. As a result, corporate earnings per share plunged from $4.80 in 1982 to $2.81 in 1983 and $2.92 in 1985. Return on assets for corn wet-milling reached an all-time low of 2.8% in 1985.

While much of this decline could be dismissed as a "bookkeeping" adjustment, it was nevertheless a recognition, with the benefit of hindsight, that the earnings in corn wet-milling in previous years had been overstated because of understated depreciation charges on outdated plant facilities.

Throughout this difficult period the public position of the company continued to be one of sustained confidence in the long-term benefits of the $1.5 billion Investment for Growth program, which persisted in both corn wet-milling and grocery product operations through 1989. A significant increase in debt servicing ($20 million) occurred in 1984 from new funding of the investment program. The strong tradition of financial conservatism that had been the hallmark of CPC was being put to work (CPC was once called The Bank That Grinds Corn).

The impact of this sudden decline in performance on the financial community was heard in 1986 in a rising chorus of analysts calling for major restructuring of CPC. The goal of an "equitable" return to stockholders by "doing better what you do best" inevitably provoked the question, Was its best good enough? The analysts, on behalf of the stockholders, were saying an emphatic no.

Two Decades of Structuring, a Year of Restructuring

The analysts' chorus was quickly followed by a solo performance by Ronald O. Perelman. Starting on October 14, 1986, a

Perelman investor group began to accumulate CPC shares.[9] Perelman, chairman of Revlon Inc., was a self-styled corporate makeover artist. How and why CPC appeared on Perelman's screen is not known, but it is clear from Table 8.3 that it was only one of many prospective targets, not only of Perelman but undoubtedly of others as well.

The CPC response first became apparent to the investing public on November 4, when the company announced that it had engaged Salomon Brothers to provide independent evidence on the value of CPC equity and to advise on a restructuring strategy. This had been initiated prior to the Perelman intervention. As often happens, Wall Street would willingly serve two masters, for both attack and defense. The first response announced the same day was a plan to repurchase 20% of its common stock (10 million of 48.7 million shares), thus further stimulating the price of the stock and making a takeover more expensive. McKee had always opposed stock repurchase: "Why reduce capital in a capital-short world?" Two days later, CPC announced that it had purchased from Salomon Brothers 4 million shares, 3.7 million of which were owned by the Perelman group. The purchase immediately deflated takeover expectations and caused a same-day decline in the price of CPC common of almost 9%. Amid angry cries of "greenmail" from arbitrageurs, the company vehemently denied the charge, defended its arm's-length relationship with Salomon, and offered as proof that the purchase of the Perelman stock was not at a premium from its market price.

Regardless, the effect was to remove the immediate threat of a challenge to control. Despite this, the sudden acceleration of change continued. On November 18, the company announced a new "shareholder rights" plan, commonly called a poison pill, which would be triggered if an outsider accumulated a 20% stake and release new stock to existing shareholders at half price.

On November 20, CPC announced that it was putting its troubled European corn wet-milling business up for sale. This was the long-awaited move, the immediate incentive for which was the repayment of the debt needed to repurchase common stock. By the end of 1986 the number of shares had been reduced by 14.6 million and by the end of 1987 by an additional 2.8 million. In the 1986–1987 restructuring, debt was temporarily increased from $800 million to

[9] Alan S. Greditor, "CPC International," *Drexel Burnham Lambert Analysts Report*, November 10, 1986, p. 25.

Table 8.3 Perelman's Route to the Big Leagues

Company (Percent owned)	Business	Year	Investment ($ millions)	Action
Cohen-Hatfield Industries (40%)	Jewelry retailer	1978	$1.7	Sold jewelry business for $8 million
Macandrews & Forbes (100%)	Licorice extract, chocolate	1980	47	Sold chocolate business this year for $41 million
Technicolor (100%)	Film processing	1982	120[a]	Sold four divisions, real estate, for $68 million
Consolidated Cigar (100%)	Cigars	1984	104[a]	Expanded operations
Video Corp. of America (100%)	Videocassettes	1985	35	Merged with Technicolor's videocassette unit
Pantry Pride[b] (cash)	Supermarkets, drugstores	1985	90	Raised $200 million in asset sales; used to buy Revlon
Revlon Inc. (100%)	Cosmetics, health care	1985	1,800	Gained $1.6 billion from asset sales
Transworld (15%)	Hotels, restaurants	1986	223	Won option to buy Hilton International for $1 billion
CPC International (8%)	Food processing	1986	325	Sold stake to Salomon Brothers for gain of $41 million
Gillette Co. (14%)	Razors, toiletries	1986	4,100[c]	Made cash acquisition offer

[a] Includes assumption of debt.
[b] Holding Co. name changed to Revlon Group Inc.
[c] Proposed.

(Data: Revlon Group Inc., BW Estimates)

Source: Reprinted from December 1, 1986 issue of *Business Week* (p. 110) by special permission, copyright © 1986 by McGraw-Hill, Inc.

$1.7 billion, raising the debt-to-capitalization (debt-plus-equity) ratio to 65% from 30%. This debt burden made a traditionally conservative institution very nervous and heightened the pressure to dispose of significant assets quickly.

In March 1987, it was announced that an agreement to sell the European corn wet-milling business had been reached. The buyer was an aggressive growth-minded Italian food and agriculture group, Ferruzzi, which would pay $600 million for the business. The purchase would make Ferruzzi the largest European producer of starch.[10] Three weeks earlier CPC had reported an agreement to sell its half interest in a Japanese food business and a 50% stake in other Asian businesses to Ajinomoto Company of Japan for $340 million. To insiders, the sale of the European business was no surprise, but the sale of the Japanese and Asian businesses was a distinct shock. These were among the company's most successful and profitable activities. Under the pressure of involuntary restructuring, even the crown jewels are not safe. The need for cash and the ready marketability of an asset are compelling motivations. It was reported by an insider that from a purely investment viewpoint, the Japanese sale made eminent good sense. The market multiple of business earnings was so strong in an overheated Japanese economy, and the restrictions on foreign withdrawal of funds so onerous, that the effective yield (cash on cash at market value) was well below comparable investment alternatives. But to those who had built the business over many years in a tough competitive market it was "like selling your own child." It is an interesting observation that it was those investments at both extremes of profitability—very low and very high—which become vulnerable to the rush to restructure. This was not unique to the CPC experience.

There were other components of the restructuring program. Other divestments, as well as some acquisitions, were made. The most notable acquisition occurred in November 1986, when CPC purchased Arnold Food Company, which added significantly to the baked goods division of S.B. Thomas.

In summary, the key aspects of restructuring were

1. a major reduction in the amount of discretionary funds by disbursement of cash to shareholders through increased dividends and stock repurchase, thus reducing the denominator of ROE.
2. a new cash-management discipline imposed by high levels of

[10] *The Financial Times*, London, March 24, 1987, p. 1.

debt servicing, which was perceived as threatening to flexibility if not to solvency.

3. a new emphasis on return on investment, which produced a clear commitment to branded grocery products as the primary means of future growth and profitability. The grocery business was then 80% of company revenues. ROE was thus immediately enhanced. Significantly, CPC discontinued its corn wet-milling research facility (and the art deco building it occupied was gifted to the Illinois Institute of Technology), thus signaling a shift to a "harvesting mode." Barring a major change in the competitive environment and profitability of the business, CPC had probably seen its last major Investment for Growth program in U.S. corn wet-milling.

The Results of Restructuring

James Eiszner, appointed chief executive in 1984 at the age of 56, had the misfortune to inherit corporate leadership just in time to receive the full impact of the capital market's pent-up impatience with the pace of structural change at CPC. In 1965, when CPC acquired the Ott Chemical Company (which it later divested), Eiszner, who had been its head, was one of the assets. With a doctorate in organic chemistry, he began his career as a research chemist. At CPC he had become senior vice president of marketing and sales for the U.S. industrial division, later corporate vice president, and then president of this division. He had been the corporation's president and chief operating officer since 1979 and a member of the board since 1975.[11]

Triggered by the Perelman raid, Eiszner responded with an all-out restructuring plan that he pursued with unrelenting speed and intensity. Management had clearly got the message. An "equitable return to shareholders" had become "Foremost among our objectives . . . : to increase stockholder values." The results were apparent within twelve months.

- 1987 net income rose 62% to $354.8 million, including a special gain of $126 million.
- Earnings per share of $4.34 were 89% higher than in 1986. Excluding

[11] *The Wall Street Journal*, June 21, 1984, p. 53.

Table 8.4 CPC Financial Performance Analysis

			1989	1988	1987	1986	1985
Return on Sales	=	$\dfrac{\text{Earnings}}{\text{Sales}}$	6.42%	6.15%	7.24%	4.82%	3.37%
× Asset Turnover	=	$\dfrac{\text{Sales}}{\text{Assets}}$	1.53x	1.44x	1.34x	1.51x	1.57x
= Return on Assets	=	$\dfrac{\text{Earnings}}{\text{Assets}}$	9.8%	8.9%	9.7%	7.3%	5.3%
× Assets/Equity Ratio	=	$\dfrac{\text{Assets}}{\text{Equity}}$	2.77x	2.86x	3.57x	2.59x	1.99x
= Return on Stock-holders' Equity		$\dfrac{\text{Earnings}}{\text{Equity}}$	27.2%	25.3%	34.7%	18.8%	10.5%

Note: The years 1987 and 1985 include the effects of special items; 1987 data benefited from a one-time gain of $176 million from restructuring activities.

Source: CPC *Annual Report,* 1989, p. 23.

the special gain, earnings per share were up 22% to $2.80 in 1987 from $2.30 in 1986.

- Operating income rose 54% to $666.4 million. Excluding the special gain, operating income was 13.5% higher than in 1986.
- Continuing operations—excluding from 1987 and 1986 results the sales and earnings of operations sold in 1987—showed gains of 33% in operating income and 19% in sales.[12]

By the end of 1989 there were substantial improvements in return on investment, as shown in Table 8.4. Return on sales, excluding special items, continued to suffer in 1987 from a declining European corn wet-milling business before its sale to Ferruzzi. Then the underlying ROS rebounded dramatically in 1988 and 1989. It is to be noted also that return on equity continued to rise beyond 1987 despite a sharp reduction in the debt multiplier from its peak in 1987 at the time of the stock repurchase. Capital expenditures had declined 50% since their peak in 1985, while advertising expenses had risen 78%, a sign of the shift away from capital-intensive to marketing-intensive industries.

At the peak of a successful turnaround, James R. Eiszner resigned as chief executive officer of CPC in August 1990 and died in September of that year at the age of 63.

[12] CPC International, *Annual Report,* 1987, pp. 2–3.

Two Decades of Performance

To give a clear idea of the impact of restructuring at CPC and the comparative performance of the McKee and Eiszner eras, I present three sets of data. The first is the corporate rate of return on sales and on equity for the decades of the 1970s and 1980s (see Figure 8.1). The second is the market-to-book-value ratio (common stock) for CPC, a group of comparable companies in the food industry, and the Standard & Poor's 500 index (see Figure 8.2). This ratio tracks the mood of market optimism or pessimism regarding corporate reinvestment for the future. The third is total shareholder return, as provided for the other two companies in Part II (see Figure 8.3). Collectively, these indices reveal the record of performance and the signals being transmitted to a chief executive regarding the corporate and market response to his strategic leadership.

From 1972 to 1982 there was a modest but persistent upward trend in return on equity at CPC (Figure 8.1). It should be noted that the relative improvement in return on sales (ROS) from 1974 to 1982 was stronger than the return on equity (ROE), and therefore that ROE was weakened by the fact of a declining balance sheet multiplier

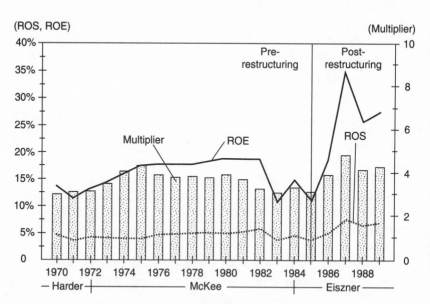

Figure 8.1   CPC International Returns on Sales and Equity

Source: CPC annual reports.

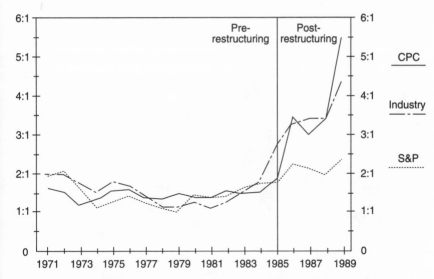

Figure 8.2   CPC International Market-to-Book Ratios

Source: Standard and Poor's COMPUSTAT.

through this period. Management's handling of asset and debt structure was less aggressive than previously, which hurt ROE improvement. On the whole, though there is always cause for hope to do
better, McKee should have been encouraged by these trends, which
reinforced the success previously mentioned in steadily improving
earnings per share. It was only in 1983—one year before his retirement as CEO, that the warning flag went up, with a sharp decline
in both ROE and ROS.

Figure 8.2 shows the market-to-book value ratios. Except for the
years 1973 to 1975, there was no dramatic or sustained improvement
in the ratio under McKee's leadership as it hovered in a range around
1.3 to 1.5. Each dollar of new investment by CPC was being valued
at about $1.40, an apparent encouragement to reinvest.

More important, however, is the comparison to companies in the
same industry considered as roughly comparable investments, and to
industry as a whole. When he took over, McKee found CPC lagging
both direct competitors and industry in general in terms of the market
multiple. By 1974, CPC had surpassed the S&P 500 companies and,
by 1978, its food industry competitors. It was not until 1983 that
these relationships reversed. So, here also, the signals from the rank

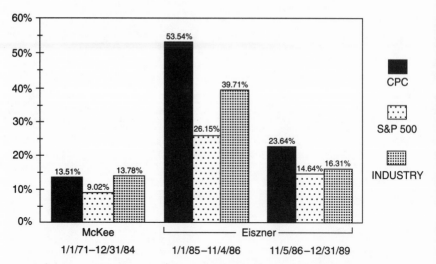

Figure 8.3   CPC International Annual Rate of Return to Shareholders (compared to the industry and the S&P 500)

Note: November 4, 1986, is the date of CPC's initial response to the takeover attempt.
Source: Center for Research on Security Prices (University of Chicago).

and file of investors would have lent positive support to the McKee leadership up to one year before his retirement.

Looking beyond to the restructuring under James Eiszner, which got under way in 1986, it is apparent from Figures 8.1 and 8.2 that there was a dramatic improvement in both ROS and ROE and a strong market response in a rising market-to-book ratio for the common stock. By 1989, shareholders were attaching an astonishing $5.50 of market value to each $1.00 of book-value accumulation.

Figure 8.3 shows the payoff to investors who held CPC common stock during the McKee and Eiszner eras. The figure shows the average annual rate of return on investment from capital gains plus dividends. If McKee had been tracking these numbers, with no further knowledge of subsequent events, he probably would have been reassured by the fact that he matched the industry average and beat the S&P 500 by a wide margin of 4.5%.

The Eiszner era is broken into two parts: the short period from the date of his appointment to the first public move to restructure, and the balance of his term under a strong restructuring initiative. The dramatic increase in shareholder returns prior to restructuring resulted primarily from market expectations associated with the Perelman raid. The period since the Perelman buyout and subsequent restructuring showed a more modest improvement but still almost double that of the McKee era. In both parts of the Eiszner era, CPC returns exceeded both the industry and the S&P by a wide margin. The case for restructuring, at least from the stockholders' viewpoint, appears conclusive.

CPC Restructuring—Voluntary or Involuntary?

One of the points made in Chapter 3 was the apparent necessity for clear and persuasive evidence of imminent danger to the corporate entity or its management to precipitate a radical change in direction. The first warning signal at CPC—the sudden and sharp downturn in return on investment—came too late for McKee and, apparently, too early for Eiszner, who was just beginning to establish his own leadership. The second signal—the Perelman raid—was unmistakable and undeniable.

By definition, the CPC restructuring cannot be classed as voluntary since, although it was successfully implemented by incumbent management, it occurred under a direct threat of investor intervention. There can be no doubt that the primary elements of the restructuring had in fact been seriously considered over a number of years and had their active supporters within the management team. However, the key element, the withdrawal of investment from corn wet-milling, was difficult for two successive CEOs to accept. This was perhaps not surprising since each had built his own management identity within the industry. Had the board seen the issue clearly, it might have seized the opportunity of McKee's retirement to choose a replacement unencumbered by commitments to the industrial commodity product line. There is no public information to indicate that the issue was seriously considered by the board at the time.

It should be added, however, that once the need for radical restructuring was unavoidable, the many previous rehearsals of the available options and the related analysis enabled the company to move with remarkable speed to implement change. This undoubtedly had much to do with the evaporation of other possible challenges and the strongly positive market response to the actions taken.

PART III

The Management of Structural Change

CHAPTER 9

The Record of the 1980s

Chapter Overview

This chapter draws together the observations of the study, particularly as they relate to the decade of restructuring just past, and offers an opinion on the efficiency with which the American private enterprise system has responded to the need for change. Recognizing that changes in efficiency are always relative, never absolute or final, I reached the conclusion that, on the whole, the enterprises included in this study recognized, and in large measure did, what needed to be done.

In response to a reempowered and reenergized ownership constituency, these businesses trimmed back on less profitable peripheral activities, refocused on core competence, returned excess resources to the capital markets for alternative investment, managed resources more aggressively, and garnered a larger share of the value-added for the owners. There was, of course, resistance to change, as there always is when priorities change and vested interests are threatened. All business organizations represent a coalition of interests competing for the wealth-creating potential of the enterprise. There were also, on occasion, breakdowns in the system of voluntary response to change, which presented powerful incentives for hostile intervention, as some of our cases illustrate. The scene could and did get messy

159

and there were major losers as well as major winners in the process. On the whole, the system of self-discipline by a professional management corps, as judged by this sample of companies, worked reasonably well. It was not a perfect record, but the overall performance was successful in the sense that the primary economic objectives for financial restructuring in the 1980s were widely understood and largely achieved.

A Historical Perspective

Those who have offered an interpretation of the wave of financial restructuring that occurred in the 1980s—and there have been many—have in the main viewed the actions taken as an effort to right the wrongs committed by corporate management in the 1960s and 1970s. Management lost its way, and the forces of the capital market intervened to restore the proper direction. It might then be inferred that now that the right priorities have been reasserted, strategy and structure will remain dedicated to the economically correct agenda. Restructuring will have completed its essential functions.

However, as we have seen in the three case histories provided in the preceding chapters, corporate restructuring is not a once-in-a lifetime event but an unending process of adaptation to a constantly changing environment. It occurs and recurs periodically because of a persistent tension between the organizational need for stability and continuity on the one hand, and the economic necessity of adaptation to change on the other. The "wrongs" that develop during one period of stable strategy and structure are never permanently "righted" because each new restructuring becomes the platform on which the next era of stability and continuity is constructed.

Indeed, many of the businesses we have observed owe their very existence to an opportunity created by the restructuring of a product, a market, or an industry. General Mills was conceived as a means of consolidating flour milling on a national scale when only regional affiliations had existed. Burlington Northern was formed as a network of several regional rail transport systems. Corn Products was formed to exploit a new continuous corn wet-milling process for producing starch, oil, and feed. The opportunity to exploit a new competitive advantage was the defining vision of the founder and became the backbone of the company's initial strategy and structure. On this basis, the broad coalition of long-term investors, human and financial, was formed.

Inevitably, the concepts of purpose and direction that were responsible for the company's initial success were challenged by new forces of change. For General Mills it was the dislocation produced by World War II and the economic and social revolution brought on by the migration of women out of the home and into the workplace. For Burlington Northern it was the comparative advantage of alternative means of transportation and the erratic cycles in demand for alternative sources of energy. For CPC it was the maturing of a domestic and global competitive environment in a capital-intensive commodity business plagued by periodic overcapacity. In each case, it was a new chief executive who recognized a problem and responded, sometimes belatedly and reluctantly, with a bold new strategy and structure.

Along with these long-term environmental shifts there were a series of initiatives taken by or on behalf of various corporate constituencies, in part stimulated and empowered by environmental change, which had important consequences for how a company's assets and liabilities were structured and how the cash flows were distributed. For consumers there was the rise of antitrust action in the post–World War II period, which drove leading corporations to achieve further growth through diversification outside their primary industry and overseas, and its subsequent decline during the 1980s and the Ronald Reagan years, making industry consolidation more acceptable. For the work force there was the competition for scarce human resources in a buoyant economy, which produced wage gains in excess of the cost of living, strong unions, job security, pensions, medical benefits—once gained, then reinforced by government regulation and oversight. There was also the decline of union influence as the balance of the work force changed and competitiveness eroded, partly, it was alleged, by an inflated compensation package out of line with the competition, domestic or international.

For investors there were the regulation and deregulation of the capital markets and financial institutions, which strongly influenced the accumulation and distribution of capital and the risk/reward incentives that were so important in empowering the challenge to incumbent management in the 1980s. For the general public, local and national, there were civil rights movements, consumer protection, environmentalism, and of course, deficit spending and tax revision, all of which bore directly or indirectly on how the corporate revenue stream was disbursed.

These and other forces bearing on the established strategy and structure at times produced a collective momentum that suggested the possibility of, if not the necessity for, radical, nationwide restructuring. Certain constituencies advantaged by environmental change meant that other constituencies, and perhaps the corporation itself, were perceiving themselves as increasingly disadvantaged. This was the case of the equity investor in the late 1970s and early 1980s.

The Consequences of the 1980s Restructuring

There were three distinct, but related, consequences of the changes in strategy and structure widely adopted by corporate America during the 1980s. The first was the rejection of the concept of unrelated product-market diversification, the extreme form of which was the unrestrained conglomerate enterprise. In its place, the new concept was a return to the core competence of the enterprise and the shedding of all corporate activity which did not draw heavily on that core competence. In capital-market jargon, it was a return to "pure plays."

The second consequence of the 1980s was the abandonment of the concept of financial self-sufficiency—of the firm as its own internal capital market, largely independent of the external (public) debt and equity markets for the funding of new investment. It was a concept related to the goal of product-market diversification but related also to conservative debt policy and heavy reliance on retained earnings and accumulated reserves.

The third consequence—not unique to the 1980s—was progress (or lack of it) on the persistent need for renewal of the primary source of long-term earning capacity of the enterprise. Some of the businesses we have observed have been locked into mature products, markets, and technologies that have persistently frustrated managements seeking a secure basis for long-term growth and profitability. If the core of the enterprise has these characteristics, a return to the core has an ominous ring to it. Long-term and even short-term survival hang on the success of a renewal process, and one is struck by the sharp contrast between the restructuring of those companies in which the core remained healthy (General Mills) and those in which it was seriously impaired (Armco).

Chapter 2 explained the foundation of the drive for diversification of product markets and revenue streams. These forms of financial strategy and structure were widely and uncritically accepted at the time and became a central theme of the then current theory of best management practice. Perhaps the best example was the well-known Boston Consulting Group product portfolio two-by-two matrix of cash generation and use in which infant market positions were fed by mature market positions ("cash cows").[1] All this was changed in the 1980s. The concept of self-sustaining growth continues to be an essential concept for small privately financed enterprise but is now out of date for the public corporation.

What changed was the rejection of the idea that the public corporation should be insulated from the discipline of the capital markets that is imposed when the company is required to come to the equity and debt markets on a regular basis for new infusions of long-term investment capital. This discipline is reimposed when the internal capital market is broken up, peripheral business entities are sold or spun off, and the company returns to its traditional or redefined core business. We saw this when General Mills sold off the toy and fashion businesses, among others, and went back to concentrating on its historic strength in consumer foods. We also saw it when Burlington Northern split off the resources business from the railroad and when CPC divested its European corn wet-milling business.

In the process, inefficient market positions were no longer sustained indefinitely by their more successful corporate siblings and were released, either to survive independently in the marketplace or be absorbed by larger, more efficient companies in the same industry. General Mills' Kenner Parker toys division survived quite successfully for a time as an independent company, but was eventually absorbed by Tonka. An important side effect of this disaggregation process for investors was that financial information was also disaggregated and the market got a better insight into the unique financial condition of each company.

During the period when many companies were pursuing their particular conglomerate strategy, the core business was going through a transformation, surrounded and obscured by the cocoon of diversified business segments. Household International entered its conglomerate phase as a national mass marketer of consumer loans and emerged as a diversified financial services company. In contrast, American Can began in the manufacture and lease of equipment for

[1] See J.B. Quinn, H. Mintzberg, and R.M. James, *The Strategy Process* (Englewood Cliffs, N.J.: Prentice-Hall, 1988), p. 600.

making three-piece cans, missed the revolution in can technology and instead evolved through paper and plastic packaging to specialty retailing, and finally emerged as a financial services company engaged in insurance, mutual funds, mortgage banking, and brokerage. Little remained of the original company except a fragment of the original name, Primerica. Armco, on the other hand, began as a steel company, flirted dangerously with insurance, and emerged as a smaller, refocused steel company once again.

In Chapter 10 we will look at the future of corporate diversification. More than one company looked back on the 1960s and 1970s and explained that they had "lost their way," i.e., their unique product-market identity. If so, the 1980s were a time for rediscovery of that identity, to the general benefit of the economy.

In addition to the benefit from a more narrowly defined and reenergized product-market mission, the release of excess funds from overcapitalized balance sheets benefited the economy by allowing such funds to seek their most profitable use. The repurchase of stock and increased dividends were the means by which this was accomplished. While the motive in some cases may have been self-preservation, by removing one of the motives for hostile takeovers, the results were nevertheless beneficial in forcing a more aggressive cash management of remaining resources.

The impact of restructuring on the mix of corporate funding between debt and equity was of more questionable benefit. One of the effects of the post–Great Depression swing to deep financial conservatism by many companies, as evidenced by triple-A bond ratings and negligible debt-equity ratios, was to reduce the influence of long-term lenders on the strategic direction of enterprise. Those of us who served on corporate boards when bankers were more frequent fellow board members recall the persistent concerns of a representative of the long-term investor. The Burlington Northern example of a leadership change is a unique illustration of that influence. With the disappearance of the equity investor in the person of the founder or his heirs, noted in several of the companies in this study, and their replacement by anonymous, transient investment institutions, these boards lost the single-minded investor viewpoint and, perhaps, their defense against unfocused investment.

On the other hand, going from one extreme to the other is hardly the solution. The dramatic run-up of the debt-equity ratio resulting from the substitution of debt for equity as a defensive redistribution of invested capital, which we saw in cases like Martin Marietta, Safeway, and CPC, imposed an unsustainable debt-servicing burden that could be met only in the short term by asset liquidation (or, as in the case of Martin Marietta, in combination with the subsequent issuance of new preferred and common equity). The first order of business was to get the debt burden back down to levels that could be supported by continuing operations. The defensive maneuver of highly leveraged transactions can produce a level of financial risk which no management would tolerate under normal circumstances. In following that path, management is betting on the probability of a subsequent period of sustained cash flow for however many months or years it takes to return debt to normal levels. Meanwhile, myopic or dysfunctional cash management may neglect everything but the most urgent short-term expenditures. As a result, a window of strategic advantage may open to competitors if they choose to act at a moment of weakness.

Overall, however, these consequences of the restructuring of the 1980s were healthy for the economy. In recent years, much has been made of the breakdown of U.S. competitiveness in global markets, attributed, partially at least, to a preoccupation with quarter-to-quarter performance and lack of commitment to long-term investment. This study suggests an alternative explanation to that of simple investment myopia.

It posits that by following a strategy of diversification and financial self-sufficiency, the corporate enterprise insulated itself from the discipline of both the product and capital markets and as a result became less sensitive to the competitive demands for long-term survival in any of its individual product-market positions. Competitive weakness in an individual product market, which would not have been tolerated in a stand-alone enterprise dependent on public capital, was often tolerated and sustained by infusions of capital from other, more successful product-market affiliates. On a stand-alone basis the unit would have found a way to succeed, have failed, or been merged with a more successful enterprise.

The primary thrust of restructuring in the 1980s was therefore to expose individual product-market positions to the competitive forces of their own product and capital markets—domestic and foreign—and in the process the fittest would survive and prosper.

Winners and Losers

In presenting new initiatives to those who are affected by them, management is fond of characterizing the intended results as a "win-win" opportunity. Major restructuring is not one of those initiatives. When the structure of investment and the payoffs from investment are substantially and permanently changed, there are bound to be some losers.

First, who were the winners? The intended winners in the capital-market-induced restructuring of the 1980s were obviously the shareholders. Judging by the case history data illustrated in this study, they obviously expected to win "big"—and did win if they cashed in on the run-up of market value of their securities after restructuring initiatives. Other aggregate studies of these data confirm this view.[2]

It was not, however, just a matter of expectations. At a more important and fundamental level, the rate of profitability was substantially and persistently improved, as the data have shown. The capital market as a whole benefited from cleaner and clearer investment choices, better information, more efficient use of surplus funds, more choice over the use of those funds.

The entire capital market was not uniformly pleased, however, because what benefited shareholders, at times, seriously disadvantaged bondholders. Bondholders who through the 1960s and 1970s had enjoyed predictable returns at minimal risk suddenly found their risk raised and their priority downgraded as the junk bond invasion hit the balance sheets of many previously respectable corporations. Changes in the sources and quality of earnings could and did occur overnight, and some lenders faced substantial loss of value of their securities. The reader is reminded of the protest lodged by the bond analyst regarding Burlington Northern's split-up and allocation of the corporate debt (Chapter 7). Her fears were not unfounded. The Burlington Northern bond ratings (S&P) went from AA in the third quarter of 1988 to BBB+ in the fourth quarter and have remained there since. The world of the bondholder had become more uncertain.

And the advantage to equity holders was not entirely unalloyed. There were higher rates of return, but these were often on increased risk, and the risk-adjusted return was unspecified. The risk increased for three primary reasons. First, the earnings obtained from a less diversified earnings base (the refocused core business) did not have the cushioning effect of possible offsetting movements among associated product markets. They could be more variable. Second,

[2] See, for example, Michael C. Jensen, "The Takeover Controversy: Analysis and Evidence," *Midland Corporate Finance Journal*, vol. 4, no. 2, Summer 1986, Table 2, pp. 30–31.

the companies were stripped of excess reserves that provided cash-flow staying power in periods of economic distress. Third, as mentioned earlier, the risk of excess leverage could be great for some companies engaged in emergency defensive action. Taken together, better returns were frequently accompanied by higher risk and, in the extreme, the risk of bankruptcy.

The primary losers in the restructuring of the 1980s were the long-term investors of human capital who had made a career commitment to an enterprise in the expectation that the strategy and structure in place at the time of permanent employment would remain for a lifetime. A reading of history would demonstrate that to be a false assumption: a single decade of stability is, in practice, about the best one can hope for. For many companies, the continuity of strategy through most of the 1960s and 1970s gave a misleading impression that retirement could be reached without disruption.

Taking examples from the companies included in this study, the losers were:

1. the United Steel Workers at American Alloys who took a cut in wages and benefits from $20 an hour to $14 an hour and those who were made redundant by reorganization of the work force.
2. the 300 word processors at Safeway headquarters who were out of work because of the elimination of an entire word-processing department.
3. the two-income families of employees at the headquarters of Burlington Northern or Armco where, when it was announced that corporate headquarters was to be relocated to another city, faced the choice—if they had one—of whose job they would give up.
4. the senior employees at all levels of the organization who were the target of widespread downsizing and faced the prospect of either loss of job or an early retirement package worth less than the present value of their remaining salary and benefits.
5. the layers of middle management who discovered that management oversight, information, and control had, after all they had been taught in business school, an ill-defined and tenuous relationship to profitability, which could be dispensed with to produce a positive impact on the bottom line.

Top management will say with total conviction that these sacrifices were mandated by new standards of corporate efficiency and profitability imposed by the party in power—the owners of the corporate equity, or their surrogates. To describe segments of the corporate work force as among the losers who made the winnings possible is to state a fact, not an opinion or judgment. After all, the private enterprise system is not a federal entitlement program. And of course, some employees gained—those who remained and benefited from a more competitive enterprise with a clearer sense of competitive mission. New incentive systems meant that some not only had extended job security but also increased compensation, although that was normally tied to targets of improved performance.

There were other losers as well, as the American Alloys example makes plain—suppliers, host communities, taxpayers, and occasionally, customers who had benefited from products or services provided at uneconomic rates of return.

Taken as a whole, the restructuring of the 1980s was a necessary adjustment to correct a fundamental divergence between corporate strategy and structure and the environment of the late twentieth-century product and capital markets. The economic pain inflicted arose primarily from the sudden imposition of long-overdue change and the shattered expectations of those who had come to rely on the strategy in place. And, as always happens, some excesses and mistakes occurred in the process.

Resistance to Change/Windows of Opportunity

In the light of the obvious reality of persistent environmental change, it is natural to wonder why the typical mature business organization does not engage in continuous restructuring by an open-ended series of small, localized adjustments rather than widely spaced, companywide radical redirection. The answer is not a simple one, but this study suggests that the reasons why corporate restructuring appears as a randomly spaced radical event which tends to occur at decade-length intervals include

- the inherent uncertainty and unpredictability of business experience;
- the lengthy time frame involved in the development of a distinctive corporate strategy: in conceiving, communicating, gaining, and maintaining commitment, and implementing and adjusting to competitive response;

- the inevitable resistance to change on the part of the coalition of corporate constituencies formed to implement the established strategy, each with a vested interest in its success;
- the fact that strategic direction is strongly influenced by the peculiar experience, abilities, and foresight of individual corporate leaders; most chief executives have only one shot at implementing their unique vision of what the strategic direction should be;
- the natural tendency to respond to early adverse results by redoubling the effort to make the chosen strategy work.

In sum, it is inherent in the strategic leadership of large-scale enterprises that, despite persistent uncertainty, choices must be made and action taken on the basis of a stable set of environmental assumptions. As in theory, so in practice certain variables must be held to be constant in order to articulate, and implement, a specific and credible course of action. Effective leadership demands unqualified confidence and commitment. Thus, inevitably, some corporate strategies and structures come to be increasingly at odds with the corporate environment, creating windows of vulnerability for some—and opportunity for others. In the case of General Mills, vulnerability resulted from James McFarland's strategy of unrelated diversification, a popular strategy in the 1960s and early 1970s that later fell out of favor with the investment community as institutional portfolio management came into full flower. At the same time there was the potential for internal dissatisfaction centering on a clash of management cultures across diverse product markets and dissimilar profit and cash-flow funding capability.

As long as the whole enterprise showed good overall performance for General Mills, the value-added potential of an alternative strategy and structure responsive to a new set of environmental realities remained in the background. In the absence of external intervention, it fell to the internal inefficiencies to manifest a problem of sufficient magnitude to confront the issue. That happened with the concurrent collapse of fashion and toys. At this point, McFarland's window of vulnerability became Bruce Atwater's window of opportunity. We have seen the result in the dramatic improvement in financial performance.

In the case of Burlington Northern, the window of vulnerability developed in the 1970s under Lou Menk. It derived in part from the industrywide problems of a regulated industry with rigid revenue and cost structures. It also derived from the central focus of Menk's leadership, which was to revitalize the railroad—the only business he knew—around the exploitation of BN's proximity to high-grade coal reserves in a period of national concern over energy self-sufficiency. Unpredictable world events and a fickle national leadership in energy policy produced a hostile environment in which to launch a major long-term investment in transportation infrastructure. The resultant dismal return on investment in the late 1970s contributed to Menk's early retirement, an event which then created a window of opportunity for his successor, Richard Bressler. Unlike the General Mills case, the turnaround was slow in coming. It took 10 years before the real payoff from a new strategy at BN, designed to exploit the undeveloped resources side of the business while rationalizing the railroad, was apparent. The spin-off of resources from the rail operations was intended to capitalize on profitability gains by offering investors a "pure play" in each enterprise.

As noted, the "ill wind" that worked to the disadvantage of the CEO who fell victim to environmental change or a flawed strategy often works to the benefit of the CEO's successor. By weakening performance and reducing investor expectations, these events effectively lower the hurdle over which subsequent success must be demonstrated. In addition, it often happened that a major investment was incurred by the prior CEO, which eroded return on equity during his tenure but became an established base for the next CEO. With the investment already made, he could demonstrate a higher return without incurring an additional funding burden. This was the case in both Burlington Northern and CPC.

In the case of CPC, the vulnerability for James McKee was the visible and persistent gap in profitability between an industrial commodity (corn derivatives) and proprietary, high-margin grocery products. The immediate window of vulnerability was the sudden sharp decline in both product lines during 1983 to 1985, which focused a spotlight on the underlying causes. When the new CEO, James Eiszner, failed to respond quickly to the need for restructuring, the situation became a window of opportunity for external corporate activists, and Ronald Perelman was the first to act. He was the classic barbarian at the gates who gave Eiszner a sudden stimulus and the organizational authority and credibility for precipitate action.

The degree of public attention given to corporate restructuring can be attributed in large measure to the huge (some would say obscene) windfalls of personal wealth garnered by managers, investors, and institutional middlemen who happened to be in the right place at the right time to seize the opportunity and to benefit from the event. The potential gain from such opportunities is in direct proportion to the degree to which the existing strategy and structure is at odds with the current and prospective corporate environment, and to the duration and intensity of resistance to change. The longer an outmoded strategy has been in place and the more entrenched and obdurate the incumbent leadership, the more negative investor expectations will be and the more the potential gain from a change in strategy and structure will be discounted in the market value of the equity. A sudden change in these expectations can release an enormous surge in market value, as we saw in the CPC case. The investor who bought the day before rumors of the Perelman initiative surfaced, and held to its fruition, was greatly enriched. Such opportunities are inherent in the nature of the discontinuous, spasmodic, and highly unpredictable timing of restructuring of the public corporation.

The Efficiency of the Voluntary Process

The observations of this study clearly document the fact that the modern industrial corporation operating under the normal internal governance process is capable of effecting a major financial and strategic restructuring resulting in measurable, sustained improvement in financial performance and in structural integrity. Further, it is capable of doing this not once, but repeatedly over the decades. General Mills, in Chapter 6, illustrates a company that has successfully evolved since its founding in 1928 through depressions and recessions, wars, market and customer transformation, radical changes in the pattern of ownership and institutional investment, overheated Wall Street and capital-market activism—and has remained competitive and healthy. Other case histories give similar testimony to the capacity for the self-renewal critical to the survival of the large-scale industrial corporation under public ownership and professional management.

However, the records are not without blemish. Managements, even in the best companies, make mistakes. General Mills under two different administrations showed signs of losing its way in the paths of unrelated diversification, from which it eventually pulled back. Some such mistakes are inevitable as leaders drawn from one particular base of experience seek to chart a new course through an evolving and uncertain environment. The key to survival was the preservation and persistent renewal of the core of competitive advantage in the primary product markets, despite the distractions of what turned out to be unproductive and misdirected investment elsewhere.

Of course, critics of the voluntary process, granting that human error is inevitably part of the management process, nevertheless complain of the slow and uncertain pace of change which often accompanies voluntary restructuring. Burlington Northern, in Chapter 7, demonstrates why extended time frames are often required to effect fundamental change in the apportionment of the corporate revenue stream, the most critical aspect of financial restructuring. Capital-market interventionists can and often do effect major changes in investment and capital structure by executive decree, but only patient and persistent career managers can transform the income statement. And we have seen some of the downside of external intervention through sudden and accelerated change. The primary value of external intervention in corporate affairs—an essential component of the broader fabric of governance—like the primary value of an organized police force, lies in the *threat* of intervention and not the actuality, which is often late and traumatic. When a committee of capital-market vigilantes intervenes, the results are not always constructive for the target corporation.

Despite the essential ingredient of time in fundamental restructuring—the natural intervals of structural change are more normally decades rather than quarters or years—there is room to be concerned at times about the pace of voluntary restructuring. The problem lies in the focus of responsibility for the initiative for change and in the incentives to act. A review of the case histories included in this study suggests that it is rare for the chief executive who has conceived and implemented the structure and strategy in question to preside over the dismantling of his or her career accomplishment and to commit the energy, capacity for self-criticism, and renewed vision essential for another decade of rebuilding.

Hence, as we have seen, the task generally falls to a successor, the choice of whom and its timing are often strongly influenced by the predecessor in office. There have been cases where the author of a "failed" strategy has the wisdom and humility to choose a successor with an independent vision and a mandate for change. There have also been cases where he has not. It then becomes critical that the normally passive board kicks into an active oversight function to influence both timing and choice of a successor.

Though the data of this study are inadequate for confident generalization, it happened that roughly one-third of the cases studied involved a restructuring by a CEO voluntarily chosen by his predecessor, one-third in which the choice of a successor was significantly influenced by the intervention of the board or a major lending institution, and one-third by a successor under threat of external intervention. It is apparent that, in these latter cases, board or institutional oversight failed to influence either the choice of a successor or his initial direction soon enough to head off outside intervention.

In considering the efficiency of the voluntary restructuring process by large publicly owned industrial corporations in the United States, it is obvious that the words "voluntary" and "efficient" are relative terms which must be interpreted with due regard to the nature and complexity of the task in question and to the results obtained by alternative means. The inclusion of cases of involuntary restructuring was intended to provide this perspective.

However, as one gets closer to the details of these different experiences, the distinctions begin to blur. Perhaps the purest case of voluntary restructuring was that of General Mills. The CEOs who implemented restructuring over the decades since the company's inception were chosen from within corporate ranks and approved by the retiring CEO and the board. While there may have been occasional rumors of General Mills as a takeover target, particularly when other key competitors like Pillsbury were actively in play, there was no evidence of serious intent. Yet one can only speculate on how the general atmosphere of hostile intervention in corporate affairs at the time may have influenced the thinking of any chief executive. Certainly it was a topic of frequent conversation when boards met for informal discussion. In the absence of the crescendo of popular interest in restructuring by analysts and the financial press, the response may have been much slower in coming. Thus one wonders, How voluntary was "voluntary"?

On the other side, there is evidence that what, by our definition, was clearly involuntary was at times merely an acceleration of planning and action already proceeding along the same path (e.g., Safeway) but at a pace and in a form which left room for a further stimulus from hostile intervention. And, as the cases have made clear, the agenda of both voluntary and involuntary restructuring was essentially the same—primarily a matter of degree and speed rather than of objective.

The efficiency of the restructuring process, voluntary or involuntary, must be measured by the objective criteria of improved financial performance and by the response of investors as reflected in the market value of a company's stock and in the credit rating of its bonds. Previous chapters have documented the substantial gains in return on investment achieved as a result of voluntary change, and the positive response from investors. What is not measured is the opportunity cost of delay once the need for action became apparent to the formal or informal leaders of board oversight before a new chief executive with the capacity and determination for change was appointed. The failure of boards to engage in active oversight, to initiate a change in leadership, and to be actively involved in the choice of new leadership is frequent enough that modification of the norms of the corporate governance process are called for and justify the widespread attention it is receiving.

Unfinished Business

The cases have illustrated that as a result of substantial refocusing on and, in some cases, rejuvenation of the core product market and the return to a leaner and more efficient use of corporate resources, significant and sustained improvement in return on equity capital was achieved, to which the equity markets responded by placing a higher value on the firm.

However, as noted earlier, "efficiency" is a relative, not an absolute term. The actions taken by management in the 1980s suggested something short of total dedication to the new capital-market priorities. When CPC shed its corn wet-milling business in Europe, it did not, as some then suggested it should have, also shed its U.S. operations. When Household International shed its industrial merchandising and other businesses, it emerged with a highly diversified portfolio of financial services businesses. In selling off everything except its original and still highly profitable consumer foods business, General Mills continued to retain the restaurant businesses.

Similar questions as to the nature and extent of restructuring can be raised about the changes in the conservation and use of corporate funds and in the more aggressive use of debt leverage. Clearly, managements were often decidedly uncomfortable with debt levels beyond historical norms and gave high priority to their reduction, with obvious consequences for return on equity as well as for risk. With recession and downsizing continuing into the early 1990s, it remains to be seen what the consequences will be of a return to sustained prosperity on the balance sheet and income statement efficiencies gained in a period of serious belt tightening.

The next chapter presents an observation on the legacy left by the restructuring of the 1980s and on the prospects for change in the 1990s. I suggest that some of the problems which the recent restructuring was designed to address are not dead, but dormant, and that they will resurface as a new period of buoyancy in the economy releases the forces which the capital markets of the 1980s successfully suppressed.

CHAPTER 10

Issues for the 1990s

Chapter Overview

It should not be assumed that all the improvements in financial efficiency realized through the restructuring of the 1980s will persist through the 1990s. On the contrary, it is likely that they will not. There is inherent conflict, as well as commonalities of interest, between organizations and the owners of organizations, between investors in human capital and investors in financial capital. The principal causes of what are now described as the inefficiencies of the 1960s and 1970s, which produced the backlash from investors, continue to influence and motivate the thoughts and actions of one or more elements of the coalition of constituencies that make up a business enterprise.

The incentive to diversify, inherent in the instinct for long-term survival, never fully disappeared and will resurface, particularly in organizations faced with eroding profit margins and declining growth potential. The incentive to grow, and to sacrifice current returns for growth, is an essential part of every dynamic organization and of the job potential of its managers and employees. The tendency to overcapitalize and to minimize financial risk is naturally tempting in an uncertain environment when the opportunity presents itself and the critics are silent. The tendency to concede a greater share of

177

the corporate value-added to other constituencies is a natural market phenomenon in an economy that is closer to full employment and where there is greater competition for the goods and services these constituencies provide.

Thus there will continue to be cycles of financial efficiency as the pendulum of influence between current investors of human capital and past investors of human capital (i.e., savers and investors) swings back and forth over time. It can be expected, too, that restructuring will recur, as in the past, not as a continuous but as a discontinuous and convulsive process. The managerial and organizational need for stability and continuity in order to pursue a consistent competitive strategy will inevitably defer adjustment to environmental change beyond a period of reasonable doubt. Accumulated "deferred maintenance" will eventually be precipitated by one of the various triggers of change built into the system, as described earlier.

In making these predictions, I assume that the process of response to a changing environment will remain primarily voluntary. The chapter makes the case for why this is likely to be so and why, on the whole, it is a good thing. The expedient of external intervention is a necessary check and balance to the voluntary system, but it is a costly one that should be used as the exception, not the rule.

If this scenario is seen as an apology for the status quo, it is not intended as such. There is no reason why we cannot improve on the system. The previous chapter illustrated that the voluntary system is imperfect and breaks down with significant frequency. This chapter comments on the weaknesses of the current corporate governance system, and the last chapter is devoted to suggestions for improvement in the internal oversight process.

The Forces Driving Investment

The actions of 1980s equity investors in curtailing the scope of corporate investment, in shrinking the discretionary reserves, and in forcing the return of surplus funds to the direct control of the owners can be read as a vote of "no confidence" in the control exercised by professional management in the past. It is unlikely, however, that this mood of mistrust will survive a return to a healthy economy, or that the strategy and structure which the restructuring of the 1980s has produced will remain intact. After all, professional investors must in the long run place their investable funds in the custody of professional managers—they have no other choice.

In particular, the forces that have constrained investment in the 1980s with respect to diversification and growth will in the longer run be confronted with inherent organizational counterforces which cannot be suppressed indefinitely. I have made the point that one of the primary errors committed in the 1960s and 1970s was the trend to unrelated diversification of product markets, resulting in excessive fragmentation and in the perpetuation of uneconomic entry-level product-market operations. However, it is clear that we have not seen the end of corporate diversification, or even of unrelated diversification.

It is inherent in every self-perpetuating organization that it seeks to maintain a base of earnings capable of sustaining the enterprise in the long term. It is particularly true of businesses that find themselves on the downward slope of a mature industry in which it is increasingly difficult to maintain an adequate return on investment that they will begin to probe the boundaries of investment and seek new investment opportunities with greater earnings potential. It is, however, difficult, if not impossible, to implement a sudden and complete transfer of investment from one earnings base to another. Thus the typical response is to initiate diversification into a new or related product market while continuing with the old. We have seen many such examples in the case histories. Like a person crossing a stream on stepping-stones, balance is sustained by maintaining a footing on the last stone before a confident footing is reached on the next. The trouble was that many companies, having successfully diversified into a new and more promising earnings base, never lifted their foot off the last stone. Or, having unsuccessfully probed a new product-market position, proceeded to a third and a fourth stone without conceding mistakes and abandoning the unstable footing.

There is a school of thought which says companies that find themselves in a mature and declining product-market position ought to face up to reality and go out of existence. Uneconomic enterprise ought not to be perpetuated. Liquidation or bankruptcy is the Darwinian solution for economic weakness. It is, however, not surprising that corporations which by law have unlimited existence, and their career managers, continue to explore diversification as an escape into a new and more promising environment. Efforts at diversification will continue, though it is hoped with a more focused and disciplined approach to the range of options that can be successfully exploited.

Related to the instinct for long-term survival is the organizational need for growth. It is interesting how quickly many of the businesses whose initial response to restructuring was a sharp curtailment of expansion soon followed up with a renewed growth strategy. The drive to grow is the most elemental expression of the priorities of the investors of human capital, in contrast to the desire of investors of financial capital for conservation and maximum return on investment. Surges of new investment, particularly for long-term development, inevitably undermine the ROI in the near term. This tension between the priorities of different constituent interests can be expected to persist in the large-scale publicly funded enterprise.

The Propensity to Overcapitalize

One of the consequences of the 1980s restructuring for many companies was a swing from the overcapitalization of the 1970s to undercapitalization: to a deficiency of equity funding and a just-in-time funding policy. As outlined in the previous chapter, a legitimate complaint of the earlier postwar decades was the tendency of corporations to develop a high degree of financial self-sufficiency, which meant low debt levels and substantial redundancy in asset holdings. Since funding policy is a process of anticipating uncertain future needs, and the determination of appropriate risk levels is a matter of judgment and personal risk preference, there is no scientific answer to the question of the "right" amount of redundancy to build into a financial system.

As a consequence, the tendency is for funding practice to swing, over time, from one extreme to another: from overfunding to underfunding, and back again. In all aspects of financial policy, there is a predisposition to bury one's corporate financial identity in the averages—not to appear at an extreme and thus to attract attention—to conform to the norm. Hence, there is a pendulumlike secular movement in aggregate behavior. The 1980s was a time to move in the direction of undercapitalization, lean asset structure, and excessive debt. The debt was often produced by a defensive disgorgement of excess cash, with debt-equity ratios suddenly multiplied by substituting debt for equity.

We have noted the universal tendency of companies caught in this process to then give priority to cash conservation and accelerated debt reduction. Sensing unusual vulnerability, and a limited window of opportunity to restore normal debt levels, companies moved quickly. The extended period of recession that marked the end of the

1980s and the beginning of the 1990s has underlined the wisdom of that response for those which had time to recover their solvency. The recession, which has also served as a crash course in survival tactics for a new generation of senior managers, will undoubtedly condition investment and funding strategy in the next decade.

Therefore, the decade of the 1990s is likely to be marked by a renewed dedication to the minimization of financial risk, the restoration of financial reserves, and perhaps a renewed interest in financial self-sufficiency. The recession of the early 1990s cannot be compared to the Great Depression of the 1930s in its impact on the management psyche, but chief executives who have been buffeted by a strained banking system and rebellious shareholders are likely to seek the comfort of deeper corporate pockets when the opportunity recurs. The near collapse of the equity markets in 1987 and the consequent sharp decline in multiples will also have had its effect on confidence in ready access to those markets in sync with emerging corporate needs.

The Competition for Corporate Value-Added

I have recorded how the ultimate purpose of the restructuring of the 1980s was to improve the quality of investment performance and to increase the ROE, both by reducing investment and by increasing the bottom-line return to equity holders. The cases illustrate the substantial gains that were achieved in this respect. I have also noted that for there to be substantial winners there had to be substantial losers as the corporate value-added was transferred from one constituent group to another. This trend has been reinforced by the subsequent recession.

It is impossible to predict whether the circumstances that caused power to flow into the hands of the shareholders, and in particular, into the hands of equity-oriented activists operating in the market for corporate control, will recur in the near future. The public reaction to the era of junk bonds and the tarnished reputation of Wall Street middlemen suggests that time must elapse for memories to fade before there will again be free access to the more extreme forms of financial brinksmanship. The financial institutions that provided a ready market for low-grade bonds and the bridge financing associated with takeovers have undergone a severe reexamination of their loan portfolios and are unlikely to repeat that experience anytime soon. The decade of the 1990s is likely to be an era of relative financial conservatism and caution by both borrowers and lenders.

This lessening of raw financial power in the hands of would-be corporate interventionists must be balanced against the evidence of a new and persistent mood of active oversight by some institutional equity holders which, if it continues, will keep attention focused on the stockholder interest. How successful it will be in sustaining attention to current priorities remains to be seen. Experienced managers have noted, however, that it is difficult in a large organization to maintain a high level of financial discipline continuously over long periods of time, particularly when there is a return to prosperity, profitability, and full employment. Every organizational system works "better," from a management perspective, when there is a degree of slack in the system.

The comment of Peter Magowan of Safeway, that it is difficult to wring concessions from union negotiators when you are reporting record profits, is a reminder that prosperity and full employment strengthen the bargaining position of the investors of human capital. A return to full employment is likely to restore some or all of the give-up that occurred when equity holders had the upper hand. Thus, financial efficiency, from an equity holder perspective, is likely to be eroded at some time in the future, though perhaps not to the full extent of the 1960s and 1970s. In summary, the several elements of financial restructuring in the 1980s were directed at the reordering of corporate priorities, which ebb and flow with the balance of power within the business organization. The interests that produced the priorities of the 1960s and 1970s are still present and will be heard from again.

Cycles of Restructuring

Whether or not the future trend of events anticipated in the preceding pages comes to pass in the 1990s, there will be general agreement that the environment for business and industry will continue to evolve in ways that depart significantly from the past. Therefore it will be necessary to continue to adapt corporate and financial strategy and structure to these changes.

For all the reasons that have been explained, however, it is unlikely that business firms will be more successful in the future than in the past in implementing a process of timely and continuous adaptation to change. I have stressed the organizational imperative for continuity in strategy and structure to enable the development of consensus and support behind a clear and consistent corporate mission. There is a strong incentive to preserve the chosen direction once it is established, even when there are signs that challenge its contemporary validity. Only in hindsight is it apparent that change was inevitable and why continuity could not be sustained.

The pattern of alternate continuity and disruption is apparent in the case studies presented and can be further illustrated by reference to a company not previously introduced, the Sun Company, formerly Sun Oil Company. Sun Oil emerged from World War II under the umbrella of industry control by the "Seven Sisters"—the major integrated oil companies that dominated the production and marketing of oil. A senior executive of Sun has divided the post–World War II history of the industry and of Sun into four eras or "ages" of varying duration, each characterized by a unique perception of the industry environment and the opportunity set at the time.

The first period, which lasted from the end of World War II to 1970 (24 years), he has called the golden age of oil, when the price of oil remained stable, industry growth kept pace with GNP, large profits were realized, and tremendous wealth accumulation was pumped back into industry and corporate physical and financial reserves. This era came to an end with the development of the North Slope reserves, after which U.S. reserves began a continuous decline, and with the emergence of an independent and militant OPEC determined to assert political control over the price and quantity of the industrialized world's critical offshore reserves.

The second period, from 1970 to 1979, he refers to as the age of uncertainty: loss of control over reserves, price instability, threatened shortages, political instability in producing countries, and a new interest in alternative energy sources (we recall the response of Burlington Northern regarding coal during this period, for example). The response of Sun was twofold. The first was to make an organizational separation between domestic marketing and production/exploration, to recognize the imbalance between in-house demand and supply, and to put in question the automatic reinvestment of profits into owned reserves. The second was to follow an industry trend of related and unrelated diversification, which led Sun into trucking, industrial distribution, industrial coatings, and small entrepreneurial ventures. There was also an aborted attempt to gain a controlling interest in Becton Dickinson (health care products).

The "age of uncertainty" was an apparent industry response to a sudden loss of momentum in oil and a search for new avenues of growth potential. It came to an end in 1979, when the price of crude oil suddenly went from $13 to $28 to $34 a barrel. In an industry still dominated by an oil mentality, it was the signal all old-time oil executives had secretly hoped for, and it brought a resurgence of commitment to a new era for oil. The years 1979 to 1986 saw heavy reinvestment and consolidation in the industry. Of the three companies with the largest U.S. reserves, two were then foreign. Unfortunately for the industry, the surge in prices did not last, and prices resumed a slow but continuous decline in 1980. This period has been called the age of unrealized expectations.

It ended in 1986 when a third price shock sent oil prices down from $26 to $9 a barrel. Since that time, the industry has been characterized by the domination of a few large international players (the age of globalization), by concentration and specialization, with various pieces owned by different partners. Sun's response to this new environment was to split the company in two, spinning off its U.S. oil and gas exploration and production operation in a new company called Sun Exploration and Production Company, the remainder to continue as an independent refining and marketing company. It was a response we have observed elsewhere, notably in Burlington Northern. From another perspective, the period could be called the age of the institutional investor, as companies sought to disaggregate disparate investment segments that could find their independent market value.

The cycles of restructuring which Sun and the oil industry have experienced reflect the unique uncertainty and instability of a critical natural resource with unusual political and economic sensitivity. In this respect it is not typical of industry in general. However, in greater or less degree, all industries must be prepared to face periodic restructuring in the future as they have in the past, and management and a governance process must be capable of an appropriate and timely response.

The Future of Restructuring— Voluntary or Involuntary?

The principal focus of this study has been on the capacity of the modern large-scale, professionally managed business enterprise to voluntarily effect major structural change in a timely and efficient manner. The case studies have provided illustrations in which this complex and difficult task has been executed repeatedly and with exceptional skill. Of course, the words "timely" and "efficient" are relative terms and, with the benefit of hindsight, even management itself will conclude it could have been done better. As well, there are illustrations in which the system broke down and the end result was hostile external intervention. On the whole, however, were this sample assumed to be representative of the whole system, the study demonstrates a powerful instinct in modern enterprises for survival, self-renewal, and independence.

The fundamental question currently under debate concerns the extent to which professional investment managers who now dominate equity ownership should assert more direct control over the formation of strategy and structure in the companies that comprise their portfolios. Were the process of voluntary restructuring as I have defined it to continue, professional investors would refrain from intervention in direct control except as they influence the functioning of the board.

In considering possible changes in the corporate governance process, it is essential that we be informed by the experiences of the past. The observations of this study contribute important insights into the working of the system and how it is likely to perform in the future. One of these concerns the fundamental difference between the capital markets and the product markets on the dimension of efficiency and speed of response. Investors in financial assets, particularly in the United States, have become accustomed to instantaneous and frictionless reinvestment and restructuring of portfolios in response to new information or changed priorities. In contrast, investors in real assets operate in a relatively inefficient product market where a critical resource is the time necessary to effect a change in resource allocation and revenue distribution. As a result, professional investors typically lack the experience, expertise, and particularly the patience needed to manage a major corporate restructuring.

It is obvious that the resource of time is placed in the hands of one chief executive whose unique vision of the future will dominate corporate strategy as long as he or she remains in that position. Past experience suggests that the normal term of office of a new chief executive, barring ill health, obvious mismanagement, or abuse of office, is a minimum of five to ten years, during which the CEO must be allowed wide discretion—the freedom to succeed and the freedom to fail. This reality of the cycles of power in a corporation places severe constraints on the "efficiency" with which adjustment to change occurs, particularly when viewed through the eyes of the capital markets.

If used wisely, the resource of time will serve to confirm the nature of the needed change, to gain the commitment of the top management team, to carefully explore options, and particularly, to choose the timing of change for maximum benefit or minimum loss. We have noted the time-consuming process of renegotiation of constituency contracts, a matter uniquely suited to career professional managers capable of delivering on those contracts. In a number of cases this entire process has taken the greater part of a decade to bring to completion, even by leaders totally dedicated to the restructuring mission.

We have observed that it is unusual for a major change in strategy and structure to be initiated and executed by the same administration responsible for the prior strategy. It is more commonly executed by a successor, with or without the intervention of the board. Hence another reason why the voluntary process takes time—the time necessary for incumbent management to recognize the need for change and step aside, or to reach normal retirement. This is the element of the process in which the voluntary system is most vulnerable since, in the absence of a vigilant and assertive board, extended delay may occur.

The advantages we have seen when the voluntary restructuring process works well are highlighted by the experience of companies in which the voluntary system has broken down and hostile external intervention has occurred. The collapse of the time frame for restructuring, which inevitably accompanies hostile intervention, necessarily restricts options, seriously weakens bargaining position, forces action regardless of the conditions of the capital and product markets, exposes the business to competitive vulnerability and excessive financial risk. By definition, restructuring, whether voluntary or involuntary, involves an element of catch-up in a deteriorating condition. However, the convulsive response to sudden external intervention imposes severe penalties, which an orderly voluntary process can avoid or minimize.

Critics of voluntary restructuring under the internal governance system as practiced over recent decades will focus primarily on the "excessive" delays in response—some, but not all of which, I have described as inherent in the management of a product-market investment process. One further element of the voluntary process which we have recognized will also be a subject of debate. It is that, on the whole, restructuring voluntarily implemented by incumbent management is more "humane" than restructuring imposed by a new ownership group intent on maximizing equity values as quickly as possible. It is more humane to the extent that a deliberate objective of the restructuring process is to cushion the shock of the necessary changes on career employees, particularly those who are innocent victims of a changing corporate environment. The longer the lead time on change, the greater the opportunity.

Economists will argue that "humanity" has nothing to do with "efficiency" and that the pain inflicted by a sudden realignment of corporate goals is an inevitable consequence of an efficient market system operating in an uncertain environment. The humane treatment of employees is, however, an important element of efficiency in practice, as an essential ingredient of trust between management and long-term contractors of human capital. "Loyalty"—two-way loyalty—is a key building block of management authority.

The sensitivity of professional management to this issue is well illustrated by a dispute that erupted on the pages of *The Wall Street Journal* concerning the consequences for employees of the leveraged buyout of Safeway by Kohlberg, Kravis and Roberts, in which the incumbent CEO, Peter Magowan, participated. (See Chapter 3.) The article, by Susan Faludi, carried the provocative head "The Reckoning. Safeway LBO Yields Vast Profits but Exacts a Heavy Human Toll. Owner KKR Hails Efficiency."[1] It was a hard-hitting attack on the LBO vehicle for corporate restructuring and on the human cost of the severe financial discipline imposed by a heavy burden of debt servicing. In the same issue, a companion box article contrasted the restructuring of a competitor, Kroger, which continued as a public company through a leveraged recapitalization in which employees participated. The burden on employees was described as significantly less severe.

The Safeway article, based on 53 pages of interview notes with Peter Magowan, drew his angry rebuttal. His letter to the editor said in part:

Most importantly you never confronted the real question: the costs of change vs. the costs of no change. Never once did you mention the why, the primary reason for most of the changes that took place at Safeway: labor costs that were out of line, the consequences, long and short term, of those

---

[1] *The Wall Street Journal*, May 16, 1990.

costs, and the absolute business necessity in a low-margin, highly competitive industry for parity of labor costs. Safeway had to confront its major
business problem—labor costs that were so out of line with its non-union
competition that they caused a situation where 66% of the company was
either making no money or losing money.

It was this that caused the pressures for and the need for change at
Safeway. And it was this business problem, LBO or not, that had to be
solved. The bleeding had to stop. The most important effect of the LBO
was to highlight this need and provide the urgency and incentive to act
quickly.

The consequences of choosing to act are sometimes hard, and sometimes they do not fall equally across the board. But your portrait is a reflec-
tion of this in a fun house mirror. In the case of the Safeway corporate staff,
that staff had to be cut to match the smaller size of the company. There
was no alternative. Staff cuts have taken place at other major companies,
all over America, to reflect their business realities. If you write about the
consequences of such cuts, why confine yourself to LBOs? Or perhaps only
LBO staff cuts cause "a heavy human toll."[2]

Magowan's letter went on to a point-by-point rebuttal of statements
contained in the article, including the following: "Mr. Magowan con-
cedes that many of the people fired at headquarters in the summer
of 1986 were 'very good' employees. Cuts were made in a hurry, as
he said later in court deposition, so as 'to put the whole unpleasant
matter behind us as soon as possible.'" Safeway's response was:

Mr. Magowan didn't "concede" this; he volunteered it. What Ms. Faludi
has done again is to select one sentence from a long explanation of why the
cuts at corporate headquarters were necessary. What she was told was: "We
had a lot of assets to sell and had to consider other severance packages that
we would have to offer down the road . . . We didn't want to set a precedent
which we could have afforded for the 210 employees in the corporate office,
but would have bankrupted the company had it been applied to some 65,000
employees on similar terms and conditions. We might not have been able to
afford such settlements everywhere."

These references to headquarters staff illustrate the human cost
associated with restructuring, a cost that is accentuated when external
intervention sharply reduces the response time and forces deeper cuts.
Magowan is right in saying that these consequences are not unique
to LBOs. They do, however, contrast with the slower and more

considerate pace of voluntary restructuring, which Magowan himself was already well into prior to the hostile takeover attempt by the Dart Group, which precipitated the LBO defense. The key question is whether the deeper cuts were unavoidable and could have been accomplished by management without a gun to its head.[3]

In summary, it is my view that the evidence of this study clearly supports the desirability of a process of voluntary restructuring as the primary means by which the private enterprise system adapts to change. However, there is a recognized cost to dependence on voluntary response, which is made most apparent when the internal governance system breaks down. Thus the potential for external intervention by capital-market agents is needed as a last resort, the threat of which helps keep management focused on action necessary to preserve its cherished independence.

The Role of Board Oversight

Among the companies included in this study, a significant number manifested clear evidence that the board of directors played a significant role in precipitating and influencing a necessary restructuring process.[4] This evidence is contrary to a popular impression created by critics of the current corporate governance process that boards of public companies have generally failed to exercise due diligence of oversight on behalf of the interests of the constituency they are elected to represent. On the other hand, it is also evident that there were cases where a board appeared to be entirely passive in the face of mounting evidence of deteriorating performance. Clearly, voluntary restructuring, particularly the board oversight function, does not work perfectly. Looking to the 1990s, these shortfalls in the governance process cannot be ignored. The future of the internal governance process as we have known it, and of voluntary restructuring, will depend largely on the increased effectiveness of the board of directors in performing its oversight function.

To those who served on corporate boards in the 1960s and 1970s, it is not surprising that, in the atmosphere of the time, the typical

---

[3]For a full text of *The Wall Street Journal* article, the extended interview notes, and the Magowan response, see: Karen H. Wruck and Steve-Anna Stevens, "Leveraged Buyouts and Restructuring: The Case of Safeway, Inc. Media Response," #N9-192-094. Boston: Harvard Business School, 1992.

[4]The comments in this section are based not only on the findings of the study, but also on my service as a director of public companies over the past three decades.

board member perceived his or her relationship with the CEO as supportive rather than adversarial. The center of corporate initiative was clearly the chief executive—and usually, chairman—and while the legal responsibility of oversight was clear, in the absence of a crisis the opportunity or rationale for confrontation over corporate direction was not apparent. Those who persistently disagreed with the CEO on important strategic issues could easily find themselves isolated and perhaps not renominated. The alternative approach was to back off and await a time when events would force the issue.

While board members were fully aware of their legal role as representatives of the shareholders' interest, the first responsibility in that regard was to support the welfare of the enterprise as currently conceived by incumbent management. In the public company, "the shareholders" were typically a faceless, voiceless group who appeared, if at all, by sparse and random representation at the annual meeting to ask a few questions and to receive perfunctory answers. In the immediate post–World War II period, there were still a few large public companies, illustrated by some of the companies included in this study, that had prominent representation by long-term equity holders (the founding family) and long-term lenders (bankers) on the board. Eventually both disappeared and the only remaining presence was the annual proxy vote of shareholders, which typically rubber-stamped management's recommendations. Board members watched with detached amusement to see whether they or the public auditors were the primary recipients of the inevitable but invariably modest protest vote over the dividend or some other irritant.

All this changed in the 1980s. In those companies which were not the target of a stockholder revolt or takeover attempt, boards nevertheless became aware of the general mood of shareholder dissatisfaction and rising militancy. For the first time, legal liability became a serious concern, best reflected in the sharply rising costs of directors and officers' liability insurance. Though often uncomfortable with the rush to erect legal defenses against hostile takeover, board members usually went along, either out of genuine regard for the management in place or a preference for "the devil you know." Boards had little respect for the common cast of characters who masterminded corporate takeovers or for the "short term" perspective of the investment funds, which appeared to be the primary beneficiaries. Board members generally conceded that once a company was "in play," ultimate loss of control was likely if not inevitable. On the other hand, there was tangible value to the increased bargaining power over the price to be paid that takeover defenses conferred, and the shareholders were the beneficiaries.

The general effect of these changes was to make boards significantly more sensitive and responsive to the perceived priorities of the shareholder constituency. The critical question for the 1990s is whether this attitude will persist. If, as seems likely, lending institutions will not be in a hurry to rekindle the appetite for high-leverage takeovers, the primary pressure on management and boards will be absent. Unless shareholders find new ways to make their presence widely and persistently felt around the boardroom table, the previous subordination of the functions of the board to the agenda of the chief executive is likely to reappear, and the oversight function will again recede.

Since active oversight by the board is essential to its role in preserving the capacity for voluntary restructuring, thus avoiding the adverse consequences of external intervention, the lessons of the 1980s must be translated into specific means by which to strengthen the board oversight capacity. This is the subject of the last chapter.

CHAPTER 11

Doing It Better Next Time

Chapter Overview

The primary objective of this study of voluntary restructuring in the 1980s has been to learn from the experience of both successful and unsuccessful attempts at corporate self-discipline the circumstances and conditions that afford the best opportunity for an effective voluntary process. The mainstream of public reaction to the events of the 1980s registered a strong vote of no confidence in the voluntary response of the established corporate governance system. The vote was expressed in a cascade of proposals for reform from institutional investors, regulators, legal scholars, financial economists, and capital-market activists. Corporate governance has become so popular as a topic of scholarly and public comment that one wonders if anyone is still listening.

In most reform-minded reviews of the 1980s experience, the villain of the piece is identified as entrenched professional management, which has sacrificed stockholder wealth in favor of personal or corporate power and wealth. In this view, corporate well-being is purchased at the expense of inferior returns to shareholders whose funds would otherwise be invested to greater advantage elsewhere, even, perhaps, in the firm's dominant competitor. In perpetuating inferior performance, professional management is seen to have the passive

193

acquiescence, if not active support, of the board of directors. Boards have been singled out for particular scorn since they are, after all, the elected representatives of the stockholders. The criticisms of the board are familiar and go largely uncontested. At least the management has an excuse: time-honored self-interest.

Not surprisingly, this wave of criticism of the established corporate governance system has produced a broad range of proposals for reform, some of which assume the continuation of the existing governance structure and process and some a radical transformation of that structure. At the latter extreme, the continuation of the modern public corporation is put in question.

The general tone of the more radical proposals has been expressed by J.O. Light, who predicts, "The last share of publicly traded common stock owned by an individual will be sold in the year 2003, if current trends persist. This forecast may be fanciful (short-term trends never persist), but the basic direction is clear. By the turn of the century, the primacy of public stock ownership in the United States may have all but disappeared."[1]

In a companion article Michael Jensen, in apparent agreement with Light's prediction, anticipates the replacement of the public corporation by new forms of business organization such as LBO partnerships, particularly in mature, slow-growth industries. Governance dominated by a few active investors is welcomed by Jensen as a response to "the widespread waste and inefficiency of the public corporation and its inability to adapt to changing economic circumstances."[2]

Most reformers, however, take a less extreme position and assume that the public corporation will continue to exist as the dominant form of business organization, funding, and governance and therefore seek solutions to perceived weaknesses within that system. I share the latter point of view. It is founded on the conviction that professional investors, and other corporate constituencies, have no choice but to continue to rely on the voluntary response of professional managers as the primary instrument of change. The present governance system has its roots in the inevitable separation of powers between ownership and management.

[1]J.O. Light, "The Privatization of Equity," *Harvard Business Review*, vol. 67, no. 5, September–October 1989, pp. 62–63.

[2]Michael C. Jensen, "Eclipse of the Public Corporation," *Harvard Business Review*, vol. 67, no. 5, September–October 1989, p. 65.

The chapter begins with a review of some of the recent proposals for evolutionary reform of the governance system. It then presents the ideas for reform growing out of this study, prefaced by a recognition of the practical boundaries of intervention by those charged with oversight responsibility. Few if any of the ideas are entirely new but, if implemented, would substantially strengthen the oversight potential of the board and the investors they represent. In particular, the recommendations place special emphasis on the empowering potential for comprehensive, objective, and consistent information on the evolving competitive environment. An unrelenting focus on evidence of inferior performance would exert a discipline that no board or management could long ignore.

Evolutionary Reform

The flood of proposals for change in the corporate governance system covers a broad spectrum of options, with many thoughtful and insightful ideas for improvement. This section provides only a brief sampling of these ideas. Running through many of these proposals is a recognition of the potential power derived from the concentration of stock ownership of the larger industrial corporations in the hands of a relatively few large pension and investment funds. Because such funds are known to hold large positions in major corporations for extended periods of time, a behavior reinforced by the growth of index funds, they are assumed to be motivated to exercise control over inefficient management rather than simply walk away, as once they did.

For this to be effective, some sort of collective action is needed. One such proposal calls for the formation of a group of full-time, well-paid "professional directors" who could be used by institutional investors as a voice for the shareholder on selected corporate boards.[3] There are a number of reasons why this idea is unlikely to be seized on as a quick solution: organizational, legal, and practical.[4] Nevertheless, there is clear evidence that institutional investors, particularly public pension funds, have become much more involved in issues of corporate governance as a result of the growing immobility of their portfo-

[3] See S. Gilson and R. Kraakman, "Reinventing the Outside Director: Agenda for Institutional Investors," *Stanford Law Review* 43, p. 863.

[4] See A.A. Sommer, Jr., "Corporate Governance in the Nineties: Managers vs. Institutions," *University of Cincinnati Law Review* 59, p. 357.

lios and the manifest potential for value-enhancing restructuring demonstrated in the 1980s. Efforts to find an influential voice are likely to continue.

One variant on the theme of investor representation is the concept of a shareholders' advisory committee to inform individual corporate boards of investor concerns. This concept has been promoted by the California Public Employees Retirement System (CalPERS) as part of its ongoing activist role in corporate governance.[5] The idea was borrowed from the shareholders' committee in bankruptcy cases: the committee would be a focus for proposals for change which, it is hoped, would represent the consensus of major investing institutions and therefore be hard for boards to disregard.

A number of reform-minded critics of the U.S. system of corporate governance have looked abroad for a different model that would overcome the apparent myopia of corporate leadership and reassert a long-term investment horizon on boards and management. One such proposal is that of Michael Porter, who proposes the adoption of a system of ownership more like that in Germany today: "Seek long-term owners and give them a direct voice in governance . . . a small number of long-term or nearly permanent owners, thus creating a hybrid structure of a 'privately held' and publicly traded company."[6] How this would come about is not clear.

So far, we have been considering imposed solutions to persistent inefficiency in corporate management. Other approaches to a more vigilant corporate governance process would provide options for individual corporate boards to infuse new discipline into their own activities. Two examples follow. In a provocative *Harvard Business Review* article entitled "Reckoning with the Pension Fund Revolution," Peter Drucker comments on the outcome of the concentration of ownership in the hands of institutional investors.

By now, the wheel has come full circle. The pension funds are very different owners from nineteenth-century tycoons. They are not owners because they want to be owners but because they have no choice. They cannot sell. They also cannot become owner-managers. But they are owners nonetheless. As such, they have more than mere power. They have the responsibility to

[5] See J. W. Barnard, "Institutional Investors and the New Corporate Governance," *North Carolina Law Review* 69, p. 1135.

[6] Michael E. Porter, "Capital Disadvantage: America's Failing Capital Investment System," *Harvard Business Review*, vol. 70, no. 5, September–October 1992, p. 81.

ensure performance and results in America's largest and most important companies.[7]

Drucker goes on to venture the following prediction:

I suspect that in the end we shall develop a formal business-audit practice, analogous perhaps to the financial-audit practice of independent professional accounting firms. For while the business audit need not be conducted every year—every three years may be enough in most cases—it needs to be based on predetermined standards and go through a systematic evaluation of business performance: starting with mission and strategy, through marketing, innovation, productivity, people development, community relations, all the way to profitability.[8]

In response to similar concerns about responsiveness to equity investors, Elmer Johnson, a former executive and board member of General Motors, proposed several changes to revitalize the boardroom oversight function, including the creation of an outside director "ombudsman" as a kind of shadow chairman of the board.[9]

A different approach is taken by Lipton and Rosenblum.[10] In an attempt to reduce the disruptive consequences of the market for corporate control so apparent in the 1980s, they proposed a five-year term for boards with a concurrent five-year moratorium on hostile takeovers. At the end of each term there would be an audit of the past five years—similar to Drucker's concept of a business audit—a new five-year plan by management, and access by institutional investors to the nomination process for a new slate of board members.

All these proposals have one objective in common: to reinstate the capacity for oversight and control by ownership over the strategy and structure of the enterprise in which they invest, continuing a debate that had been joined 60 years ago by Adolf Berle and Gardiner Means.[11] Such attention and energy aimed at a power shift that would diminish the perceived absolute control of the office of the chief execu-

---

[7] Peter Drucker, "Reckoning with the Pension Fund Revolution," *Harvard Business Review*, vol. 69, no. 2, March–April 1991, p. 114.

[8] Ibid., p. 114.

[9] Elmer Johnson, "An Insider's Call for Outside Direction," *Harvard Business Review*, vol. 68, no. 2, March–April 1990, pp. 46–55.

[10] Martin Lipton and Steven A. Rosenblum, "A New System of Corporate Governance," *University of Chicago Law Review* 58, p. 187.

[11] Adolf A. Berle and Gardiner C. Means, *The Modern Corporation and Private Property* (New York: Macmillan, 1932).

tive officer and of its established constituency base has, of course, not gone unnoticed or unanswered.

Primarily in response to the wave of takeover activity, corporate leaders and their constituencies have taken several actions designed to preserve the established corporate power base. The corporation, as distinct from its ownership group, has a group of loyal constituencies, including a community and political base, which in many respects has a stronger sense of identification with the survival and long-term well-being of the individual corporation than the professional portfolio manager. It is not surprising, therefore, that these constituencies also felt threatened by the takeover phenomenon and were sympathetic to antitakeover defenses that helped to preserve the established governance intact. The reader is familiar with these. Of particular interest is the move by many states to recognize explicitly the right, if not the obligation, of boards to take the interests of constituencies other than shareholders into account when reaching prudent decisions on financial strategy and structure. The net effect of these measures was to relax some of the mounting pressure on boards of directors to hew to a narrow interpretation of stockholder interest.

Working within the System

At this writing it appears that the traditional corporate governance system has survived the 1980s and the aftershock of the reform movement largely intact. None of the measures of reform have received general acceptance, though the increased pressure from certain investors, particularly public pension funds, has persisted. The abandonment of the public corporation predicted by Jensen appears premature. At this point the 1990s appear to be taking shape much as preceding decades have done with respect to the *form* of corporate governance. But this does not mean that things have not changed. Self-governance has received a therapeutic shock, which we hope will reinforce its inherent capacity for an orderly response to needed change.

Perhaps the most significant and symbolic response to a changed environment for corporate governance in the aftermath of the 1980s has been the board revolt in General Motors referred to in Chapter 1. In an article written two years too soon, William Taylor recalled that in 1920 Pierre duPont, whose company owned 25% of GM stock, precipitated the resignation of GM's founder and managed the transition to a new chief executive, Alfred P. Sloan, who would lead General Motors to ascendancy in the U.S. auto industry for half a century.[12]

Taylor then contrasted this event with the rebuff received by Dale Hansen, CEO of CalPERS (which held 1% of GM stock), when he attempted to influence the decision to continue the outgoing chairman of GM as a member of its board. Had Taylor waited to write the article until the spring of 1992, he could have recorded a third episode of profound consequence, not only for General Motors but also for corporate America: the palace revolt in which an outside board member—John Smale, former CEO of Procter & Gamble—replaced the incumbent chairman and CEO—Robert Stempel—as chairman of the GM board's executive committee and forced a change in the company's president and COO.[13] Smale had led the board, particularly its outside board members, to force these management changes at a time of severe competitive and financial distress at GM.

Though there is no way to document the connection, this unusual event could not have occurred without a board preconditioned to the possibility of a successful challenge to corporate leadership, and the events of the 1980s surely emboldened boards to question their traditional passive relationship to the chief executive, serving "at his pleasure." Such shifts in attitude, in the absence of cataclysmic, triggering events, take place gradually and in subtle, often unspoken ways. To what extent the General Motors experience, and that of a few other highly visible corporations, is a harbinger of a new assertiveness by corporate boards, or simply an aberration, only time will tell. It certainly is a precedent for other boards to follow if circumstances warrant.

By focusing on voluntary restructuring, this study has provided evidence on the conditions of a corporate governance structure that are most conducive to a restructuring process which operates within the normal governance system. Operating on the assumption that, for the foreseeable future, necessary restructuring when it occurs will be predominantly voluntary, it is vital to focus attention on those conditions of the corporate internal and external environment which are most conducive to a voluntary process.

Before doing so, however, it is necessary to recognize some of

[12] William Taylor, "Can Big Owners Make a Difference?" *Harvard Business Review*, vol. 68, no. 5, September–October 1990, p. 70.

[13] *Business Week*, "The Board Revolt at G.M.," April 20, 1992, p. 30.

the practical constraints on intervention in an ongoing, "real-time" strategic management process that affect the way in which voluntary restructuring within the normal governance system may be expected to occur. Some of these constraints apply whether the intervention is voluntary or involuntary, whereas others may be breached in cases of involuntary restructuring—but at a cost that may not be immediately apparent. I take these basic constraints on intervention as "self-evident truths" which need statement only because some of the criticisms that have been made of the voluntary system appear to deny their operational importance.

The Boundaries of Intervention

Despite the fact that much of the criticism directed at corporate boards of directors for failing to exercise their proper oversight function in times of seriously impaired performance has been justified, there are legitimate reasons why board oversight, specifically board intervention, operates under substantial practical constraints. These include the following:

One Leader at a Time, One Vision at a Time

The obvious fact that human organizations can tolerate only one leader at a time means that there can be only one strategic vision at a time. This does *not* mean, however, that everyone associated with corporate leadership at any given time wholeheartedly shares that vision. Indeed, it is quite possible that there are members of the top management team, members of the board, or major investors who have serious reservations and would prefer an alternative course.

Everyone understands, however, that open dissent is disastrous to organizational commitment and competitive vigor, and consequently disagreement is either suppressed or voiced infrequently and in private. In corporate leadership, different personalities have different tolerance for dissent and, in any case, as long as they lead, their judgment must be final.

Standing the Test of Time

How long it takes before a new leader and his or her chosen strategy can be confidently pronounced a success or failure varies greatly,

depending on the nature of the industry, the competitive environment, the economy, and the unpredictable flow of specific circumstances and events. There are, however, practical reasons why the
time frame of strategic planning is long, customarily calibrated in half
decades. These reasons have little to do with confident prediction and
much more to do with the time it takes for large organizations to
mount their full momentum in a given direction and, especially, to
test the power of the competitive response.

When overlaid with the random impact of national and international economic cycles, five years of experience is often a short time
to take the full measure of a new strategic direction. It may be time
enough only to test the initial implementation and the first serious
competitive response, before the gross or fine tuning necessary to
reveal the strategy's mature potential. As previous case histories have
suggested, a decade is often the life cycle of one leader and one strategy before serious reappraisal.

So, how long the period should be during which a conscientious
board can or should suspend final judgment on the incumbent corporate leadership has no obvious answer and normally demands considerable patience.

Defining Failure

From a strict financial viewpoint, the definition of a failed strategy is
one which does not earn a competitive risk-adjusted rate of return on
the invested capital over a sustained period of time. Viewed in these
terms, there are at any given time a number of firms that have clearly
failed the test and a number that have clearly passed it. The problem
is that most businesses, most of the time, inhabit the gray area of
"the averages" and move in and out, partly because of things they do
or fail to do, partly because of things done to them. Thus there is
for them no precise definition of success and no clear and unambiguous signal of failure. While the statement of the financial criterion in
the opening sentence of this paragraph glides easily off the tongue,
every word or phrase is judgmental: What do you mean by "competitive" return, what risk, what invested capital, over what period of
time?

Given this, and the fact that boards are commonly fed on a very
selective diet of internal information on the past performance and
future potential of one company, they often find it difficult to reach

a definitive and final judgment on the success or failure of a constantly evolving plan of action. It is not surprising, therefore, that in reviewing even the small sample of companies included in this study, one finds a wide range of performance in the period immediately preceding a restructuring: from obvious financial distress at one extreme to what, by normal standards, was superior and persistent profitability at the other.

When these and other natural boundaries to intervention within the normal governance structure are considered together, they could be taken as further confirmation that the current governance process makes voluntary restructuring either unlikely or excessively delayed. However, the corporate governing board, like the judicial branch of government, is designed to provide a degree of deliberate inertia in the decision-making process affecting the rate of change. Those who would accelerate the rate of change are typically managers of financial assets, which in the modern capital market can be instantaneously repositioned in an infinite variety of portfolio configurations. This is not so in the case of real assets, which require long-term commitment from the producing constituencies that would be seriously distracted and disrupted by the constant threat of sudden intervention.

On the other hand, none of these constraints on voluntary intervention can be used to justify persistent inaction, especially in those cases where the negative trend is clear. In anticipation of the likely continuance of the established governance process in the foreseeable future, it is particularly important therefore to highlight the evidence from this study of those characteristics or circumstances which facilitate restructuring from within.

The Elements of a Responsive Governance Process

No governance system that depends primarily on voluntary response to a perceived need for fundamental restructuring performs to everyone's satisfaction—or even, on some occasions, to anyone's satisfaction. Nevertheless, some individual governance processes have clearly been more responsive, timely, and efficient than others. Thus, drawing attention to the unique characteristics of these processes provides an opportunity to make the self-governance system more efficient and less dependent on the threat of external intervention. Alertness to the opportunity for improvement is the responsibility of everyone directly or indirectly involved in the current corporate governance process. The characteristics of a responsive system are as follows.

The Allocation of Accountability

Because of the common practice of vesting in one person the dual responsibilities of chief executive and chairman of the board, the important differences in responsibility and accountability of the two offices become blurred. The chief executive is, by definition, the leader of a coalition of constituencies, the most important of which are the long-term investors of human and financial capital—the primary risk takers. In pursuit of a defined corporate mission, the CEO must necessarily gain and maintain the full commitment of *all* constituencies to the common objective, and in the process strike a balance among the competing interests and rewards to each constituency.

In this regard the CEO, his or her own rhetoric to the contrary notwithstanding, cannot place the interests of one constituency always ahead of the others, particularly the interests of the shareholders. The history of corporate restructuring described in this study documents that this is, in fact, the case. The ebb and flow of priorities between investors of human capital and investors of financial capital is the primary characteristic of change from decade to decade. To use the phraseology of economic theory, the chief executive cannot be expected to place the maximization of shareholders' wealth as the number one priority at all times.

At the same time, the shareholders can be expected to press for that objective and to demand that their elected representatives, the board, do likewise. The events of the 1980s have produced a renewed sensitivity to the shareholder interest. The goal of sustained improvement in the return to investors of financial capital, which the study has documented in demonstrated results, benefits not only shareholders but, to the extent that increased profitability is retained and wisely reinvested, the long-term investors of human capital as well. Nevertheless, there is an implicit and real tension between the tests of accountability appropriate to the board and to the chief executive.

Recent efforts of some state legislatures to broaden the constituency base of boards of directors to include the interests of "investors" other than the shareholders ("stakeholder statutes") may have the tendency to confuse the essential distinction between the executive and the oversight responsibility.[14] On the one hand, it is prudent to give boards the latitude to accommodate the broader mandate of the chief executive. On the other, the primary responsibility of boards to their unique constituency remains. As Chancellor W.T. Allen has said:

In most contexts, the director's responsibility runs in the first instance to the corporation as a wealth producing organization. Promotion of the long-term, wealth producing capacity of the enterprise inures ultimately to the benefit of the shareholders as the residual risk bearers of the firm, but it also benefits creditors, employees as a class, and the community generally.[15]

When one draws the distinction between the responsibilities and accountability of the board and the chief executive, the merit of separating the office of chairman and of chief executive becomes more apparent. The call for separation, which has been receiving increasing support as a means of strengthening the oversight capacity of the board, is meeting some response in corporate practice.[16] However, there will be strong resistance from chief executives who see the potential for mischief in divided authority. Nevertheless, the justification for a separation of accountability is clear.

An effective alternative to the preferred separation of office has been the appointment or election of a governance committee chaired by a board member other than the chief executive, which deals with the key issues of governance as they arise and whose chairman acts as board liaison with the chief executive and therefore as a shadow chairman.

Board Composition

Observation of those boards which have been most effective in influencing the course and timing of restructuring, particularly at the moment of succession to the office of CEO, suggest a rethinking of the sources from which board membership is drawn. As has been noted, timely intervention, when it occurs, is never initiated by the board as a collective body but rather by an individual board member with

[14] See, for example, W.T. Allen, chancellor, Delaware Court of Chancery, "Defining the Role of Outside Directors in an Age of Global Competition," address to Ray Garrett, Jr., Corporate Securities Law Institute, Northwestern University, April 1992.

[15] Ibid., p. 13.

[16] See Jay W. Lorsch, *Pawns or Potentates* (Boston: Harvard Business School Press, 1989), pp. 184–187.

a unique voice of authority and the motivation and determination to act. In the individual case, this has been a former CEO, a senior lender, a founder or his descendant, or a respected senior board member.

One of the reasons for the apparent decline in board oversight and justifiable intervention on behalf of an evident need for restructuring is the homogenization of board membership and the disappearance of recognized "voices of authority" on the board besides the chairman. Inevitably, founding families fade away, senior lenders have been discouraged from participation on the boards of companies to which they lend—on the whole, an unfortunate development—and, for obvious reasons, former CEOs are an uncomfortable presence.

It is a common practice today for boards to be composed of a minority of inside directors and a majority of outside members, the latter drawn from the ranks of senior or chief executives of other companies, from "experts," including academics, and from political constituencies. On such boards the independent voice of authority is likely to be another chief executive who speaks from a base of experience comparable to that of the incumbent CEO—and chairman. However, as a potential voice of dissent on behalf of the stockholder interest, the outside CEO–board member has one fatal flaw. His (or her) primary allegiance is to *his* stockholder group, not to that of the company in question. He therefore has little appetite or incentive to invest precious time and attention on what will likely be an open-ended commitment, not just to start a debate on leadership but to bring it to a meaningful conclusion. There is no payoff equal to the cost.

It is no surprise, therefore, to see that it was a *retired* CEO who took on the huge personal cost and risk of confronting the incumbent chief executive of General Motors. It would be highly beneficial to the boardrooms of corporate America if greater use was made of retired CEOs as board members who would bring their experience, maturity, objectivity, *and discretionary time* to the oversight process. With careful choice, this need not create an adversarial environment and should not be threatening to a self-confident and successful chief executive.

The Function of a Strategic Audit Committee

It is common practice for boards to set aside a day or two each year for a strategic and long-range planning review. It provides an opportunity to react to the strategic plan in place and, especially, to evaluate the input from individual members of the senior management team who are potential successors to the current CEO. However, as is appropriate, the entire agenda is firmly in the control of the chief executive, who is responsible for the success of the plan. Inevitably all the focus—the specific goals and the means and time frame by which they will be achieved—is on the future.

While this exercise is always interesting and even exciting, it involves the board at the wrong end of the strategic review. To put the matter in somewhat oversimplified terms, the future is the prerogative of the incumbent chief executive, the past the unique prerogative of the board; i.e., the board must make its judgments primarily on past performance, not future promise. The only real way for the board to influence the future materially is to replace the chief executive.

To draw an analogy from one of the industries included in this study—railroads—the role of the CEO in the customary strategic planning meeting is like the engineer of a train who invites the board for a brief visit to the cab of the lead engine to view with him the prospect of the elevated landscape that lies ahead. The board has no way of knowing whether the scene is reality or mirage. By definition, future plans always promise improved performance. In terms of strategic review, the proper place for the board is at the rear of the train in the caboose, in the role of brakeman, observing the slope of the terrain already traveled and whether in the longer term it has represented incline or decline. That evidence defines a credible baseline from which to judge the probability of future promise.

As a practical solution, I suggest the formation of a strategic audit committee of the board composed primarily of and chaired by outside board members. In concept, it is a modification of Peter Drucker's proposal for external strategic auditors akin to the current public audit function (see page 197). While potentially more influential and objective, Drucker's proposal is unlikely to be implemented in the foreseeable future, and the concept of an internal committee has more immediate promise. This committee would direct the gathering and presentation of the information needed to map past performance upon which informed judgments can be made. Once established, it could convene on, say, a regular three-year cycle or for a specific purpose, e.g., the impending retirement of the CEO.

Such a committee would need modest staff support. In this respect it is important that the process of data gathering be initiated in a period when the data are not seen as threatening to anyone. It should not be necessary, therefore, for the board to have its own analyst, but it could draw on corporate staff for this function. The role of strategic analyst is, however, a sensitive one that could at some time place the individual in the line of cross fire between management and the board.

Board Empowerment: Information

The power of a board to exercise the oversight function so as to influence the course of corporate affairs lies not in legal or organizational authority, but in access to the information that compels attention and demonstrates the need for change. If there is any one agenda item which this study lends to the governance debate more than any other, it is

- that in cases of major restructuring, voluntary or involuntary, the evidence of serious and persistent erosion of financial performance and structural integrity was clear and unambiguous for anyone with access to the data.
- that the consistent tracking and regular monitoring of this information by the board is essential to potential board intervention in the strategic process, normally at times of management succession.
- the specific content of that information.
- the existence of a forum (the proposed strategic audit committee) in which it is natural and necessary to identify and review such information periodically.

The case histories presented here illustrate both the nature and content of such information, which offers evidence that the corporation is substantially and persistently underperforming its competition in major respects. It is information that is clear, unambiguous, and in the public domain, and therefore accessible to public investors and professional analysts. It appears in a form that uses the common language of management reporting.

To be more specific, this information is best illustrated by the case histories of Chapters 6, 7, and 8. A consistent and consecutive set of data for the preceding decade should provide information on the record of investment and return on investment with respect to *all* of the following: (1) the company's own past performance, (2) the company's principal competitors in the same product market and for the industry as a whole, (3) the company's principal competitors for funds in the capital market that lie in a comparable investment-risk category, and (4) the response of investors to this performance over an extended period of time.

It may seem surprising to those unfamiliar with the internal governance process that this information is not commonly available to board members. The fact is that it is unusual for consistent information to be regularly provided by management because of either benign or deliberate neglect—as much the former as the latter. "Movers and shakers" are typically singularly uninterested in the past—for them, only the future moves and shakes. However, it is also true that when the past, particularly when viewed in a comparative and competitive context, is an embarrassment, management has little interest in bringing it to anyone's attention, especially that of the board of directors.

Instead, management normally prefers to emphasize plans for the future and make presentations regarding goals and implementation of strategies to achieve goals, which are, after all, what management is all about. Goals are by definition an optimistic assertion of the upside potential designed to overcome any shortfall of the past. However, it is accomplishment, not promise, that is the metric of board oversight. Board time and attention to monitoring executive performance should be focused primarily on the past. Usually it is not, because adequate information is not consistently provided. Even the company's own historical data are not always offered in a focused and consistent form. *The board should insist on, and be directly involved in, determining the content of such information.*

The data should be simple and straightforward and tailored to the unique characteristics of the particular industry. For an example of the type of data required for strategic monitoring of (1) company historical performance, see the CPC data on financial performance, Chapter 8, (2) competitive and industry comparison, see Figures 7.1 and 7.2, showing Burlington Northern versus Union Pacific and the railroad industry respectively, and (3) capital-market performance, see Figure 6.2, showing General Mills' equity returns versus those of the food industry and the S&P 500.

These are the types of data and the extended time frames that should come under regular board surveillance. These are the data that no board, in company with the chief executive, could persistently ignore. For a board of directors, information is at the center of its potential power.

It is curious that in all the talk about greater involvement by professional analysts and portfolio managers, no one seems to talk about the weapon of information. If the facts of poor performance are so abundantly clear to these professionals with a stake in ownership, why do they not target the individual members of the boards of offending companies and regularly confront them with the information they may be denied on the inside? In this regard it is interesting to remind the reader of Burlington Northern's Richard Bressler and his exchange of correspondence with a railroad analyst, which he shared with his board (see Chapter 7).

The Capacity for Intervention

Board oversight is a meaningless concept unless it includes a willingness to engage a management team in a serious dialogue on strategic direction and if necessary to confront an unresponsive CEO and intervene to initiate change. On the other hand, previous chapters have illustrated the fact that if product-market enterprise is to succeed, it needs extended periods of stability and continuity during which the collective investment, broadly defined, can be focused on specific economic objectives. The threat of frequent or random interruption or intervention to countermand established directives erodes morale and weakens commitment and trust. Even new CEOs, who have an implicit mandate for change, usually move cautiously in their early incumbency unless an obvious crisis is evident.

Thus the consideration of fundamental restructuring should be, and normally is, approached with proper care and caution. The essential ingredients for voluntary restructuring are convincing proof of the need for change, opportunities for near-term improvement, consensus among the board members and top management, and a visible mandate for change. Corporate activists in the field of restructuring are understandably impatient with the necessity for these conditions and despair of the time frame involved. Those accustomed to the instantaneous and continuous execution and feedback of the capital-market investment process find the product-market investment environment frustrating. This accounts for much of the persistent tension between corporate management and corporate ownership.

The issue of timing in the success of voluntary restructuring is of key importance and relates to the need for a visible mandate for change. The two most common mandates are the retirement and replacement of a chief executive and a sudden and significant deterioration in performance, particularly following a negative trend. Both pose a threat to the continuity of established initiatives and are widely apparent throughout an organization, putting it on notice of possible change. The window of opportunity is likely to open suddenly and perhaps briefly, and unless the initiative is seized, the opportunity may pass. There are always those who have a strong vested interest in the status quo and actively seek to frustrate change. A second opportunity may be long in coming, as when a retiring CEO promotes a successor in his own image.

As we have seen, however, the easy cases are those in which the need for change is suddenly and dramatically apparent. The more difficult—and more common—cases are those in which there is gradual or erratic erosion over extended periods of time and no one increment of decline is an obvious mandate for board intervention into what is normally the prerogative of the chief executive and the management team.

It is therefore necessary to elevate and legitimate a periodic dialogue between the board and the chief executive on long-term strategy and structure, not about the future promise of current plans and action, but about the present and past reality of demonstrated accomplishment. The strategic audit committee can provide a mandated cycle of review that, based on consistent and objective historical evidence, invites a genuine dialogue in which, it is hoped, consensus rather than confrontation can be the outcome.

Self-Renewal and the Need for Governance Reform

Undoubtedly these suggestions for a more responsive internal governance process capable of timely and effective structural evolution will encounter the cross fire of both critics and practitioners of the established system. Critics will be skeptical of the capacity of a "failed system" to engage in a process of self-renewal. Practitioners, specifically chief executives, will be wary of changes that encourage a proactive strategic oversight process led by outside board members and a more independent boardroom relationship.

The prospect for voluntary reform of the governance process depends on the extent to which the experience of the 1980s has had a significant and lasting impact on the corporate board's sense of vulnerability to external intervention in cases of serious structural imbalance. Enough turmoil has been created to make it credible that the traditional independence of governance of the private enterprise could be lost or substantially modified by political, legal, or institutional intervention. If so, managements as well as boards may be ready for self-imposed reform that will preserve the essential managerial discretion. The price of independence is active self-discipline.

At the moment the threat of external intervention has receded. Despite its absence, the restructuring process continues to surface in wave after wave of downsizing as corporations reach for solid footing on which to base the next recovery. Public attention is preoccupied with the more fundamental issues of national deficits, unemployment, and foreign competition. Corporate governance reform is not just on a back burner, it is off the stove. Under the circumstances, the temptation to slip back into old and familiar patterns of governance and oversight will be strong.

Yet if history is any guide, the next period of renewed economic growth will spawn new corporate strategies and structures responsive to the new environment. In time they, too, will outlive their relevance and the old issues of restructuring will reappear, undoubtedly accompanied by a renewed debate over corporate governance. When this happens, it is to be hoped that the real lessons of the 1980s will be remembered.

This experience has provided a vivid reminder that the real discipline on those who wield corporate power, management and its governing boards, derives not from formal legal or organizational structures, but from the forces of the markets in which the business enterprise exists. A firm survives only if it is able to meet the competitive demands of all its principal markets: for its products or services, for capital, and for human resources. The lesson of the 1980s was that in seeking to insulate the firm from the discipline of the capital markets, through financial self-sufficiency, and from the product markets, through diversification, management's sensitivity to the needs of those two critical constituencies had been weakened or temporarily lost. In many cases, the restructuring of the 1980s was a dramatic reversal of that trend.

Reform of the governance process will function best if it does not presume to be a substitute for market discipline. By enhancing the means by which both management and the board are fully informed on the evolving market environment, the corporate governance process will offer the best assurance that enlightened and informed self-interest will produce the appropriate response.

Appendix
Sources of Company Data

The primary data for this study were derived from the experience of 11 large and mature industrial corporations based in the United States. These companies agreed to cooperate by making their experience in the corporate and financial restructuring process accessible to me. In the final write-up of observations and conclusions, not all companies were cited by specific illustration or reference. Nevertheless, their individual cooperation and open discussion of their experience was essential to my general conclusions and confidence in the broader implications of the findings. Their assistance is greatly appreciated. A brief description of each of these companies is provided in this appendix. A twelfth company, American Alloys, which was referenced in this study, is private and not listed below.

AMERICAN CAN CO./PRIMERICA CORPORATION

Headquarters: New York, New York
Founded: 1901

Principal Products/Services*	1980	1990
Continuing businesses:	Specialty retailing	Direct mail marketing
Discontinued businesses:	Metal cans Flexible packaging Consumer products Food service	
New businesses:		Insurance Investment services Credit

Scale of Operations*	1980	1990
Gross revenues ($ millions)	$4,812	$6,190
Employees	51,000	27,600
Shareholders	102,030	34,500

*Each company's annual reports provided the principal products/services information, and Standard & Poor's COMPUSTAT was the source of the scale of operations data for all these companies, subject to modification by company officials.

ARMCO, INC.

Headquarters: Parsippany, New Jersey
Founded: 1917

Principal Products/Services	1980	1990
Continuing businesses:	Steel products Industrial products	Steel products Grinding systems
Discontinued businesses:	Oil field equipment Insurance	(now a joint venture) (up for sale—run-off obligations continue)

Scale of Operations	1980	1990
Gross revenues ($ millions)	$5,678	$1,735
Employees	59,800	9,800
Shareholders	69,600	36,290

BURLINGTON NORTHERN INC.

Headquarters: Fort Worth, Texas
Founded: 1961

Principal Products/Services	1980	1990
Continuing businesses:	Railroad Natural resources	Railroad Natural resources (now separately incorporated)
Discontinued businesses:	Airfreight Trucking	

Scale of Operations	1980	1990
Gross revenues ($ millions)	$3,954	$4,674
Employees	56,710	32,900
Shareholders	48,020	31,830

CPC INTERNATIONAL, INC.

Headquarters: Englewood Cliffs, New Jersey
Founded: 1906

Principal Products/Services	1980	1990
Continuing businesses:	Consumer foods Corn wet-milling	Consumer foods Corn wet-milling
Discontinued businesses:	Chemicals	

Scale of Operations	1980	1990
Gross revenues ($ millions)	$4,120	$5,781
Employees	40,500	35,000
Shareholders	57,000	33,260

EATON CORPORATION

Headquarters: Cleveland, Ohio
Founded: 1911

Principal Products/Services	1980	1990
Continuing businesses:	Vehicle components Electrical and electronic controls	Vehicle components Electrical and electronic controls
Discontinued businesses:	Materials handling vehicles (disc. 1982)	

Scale of Operations	1980	1990
Gross revenues ($ millions)	$3,176	$3,639
Employees	50,358[1]	36,603
Shareholders	35,071	17,892

[1]Continuing operations only.

GENERAL MILLS, INC.

Headquarters: Minneapolis, Minnesota
Founded: 1929

Principal Products/Services	1980	1990
Continuing businesses:	Consumer foods Restaurants	Consumer foods Restaurants
Discontinued businesses:	Games & toys Furniture Jewelry Footwear Luggage Apparel Specialty retailing Coins & stamps	

Scale of Operations	1980	1990
Gross revenues ($ millions)	$4,852	$7,153
Employees	71,230	108,080
Shareholders	27,700	37,530

HOUSEHOLD INTERNATIONAL, INC.

Headquarters: Prospect Heights, Illinois
Founded: 1925

Principal Products/Services	1980	1990
Continuing businesses:	Consumer credit Insurance	Consumer credit Insurance
Discontinued businesses:	Merchandising Manufacturing Car & truck rental Airline	
New businesses:		Banking Credit cards First mortgages Mortgage services

Scale of Operations	1980	1990
Gross revenues ($ millions)	$6,054	$4,320
Employees	78,000	14,400
Shareholders	28,530	15,580

MARTIN MARIETTA CORPORATION

Headquarters: Bethesda, Maryland
Founded: 1928

Principal Products/Services	1980	1990
Continuing businesses:	Aerospace Aggregates	Astronautics Aggregates
Discontinued businesses:	Cement Chemicals Aluminum	
New businesses:		Missiles Energy systems Air traffic systems

Scale of Operations	1980	1990
Gross revenues ($ millions)	$2,619	$6,126
Employees	34,650	62,000
Shareholders	52,490	37,150

PERKIN-ELMER CORPORATION

Headquarters: Norwalk, Connecticut
Founded: 1939

Principal Products/Services	1980	1990
Continuing businesses:	Analytic instruments Coating materials	Analytic instruments Coating materials
Discontinued businesses:	Minicomputers Semiconductor equipment Aerospace (U.S.) Missiles (Germany)	

Scale of Operations	1980	1990
Gross revenues ($ millions)	$996	$838
Employees	15,290	6,440
Shareholders	13,020	10,830

SAFEWAY STORES, INC.

Headquarters: Oakland, California
Founded: 1914

Principal Products/Services	1980	1990
Continuing businesses:	Food retailing	Food retailing

Scale of Operations	1980	1990
Gross revenues ($ millions)	$15,103	$14,874
Employees	150,010	114,500
Shareholders	49,790	3,660

SUN COMPANY, INC.

Headquarters: Radnor, Pennsylvania
Founded: 1901

Principal Products/Services	1980	1990
Continuing businesses:	Oil & gas Coal	Oil & gas Coal
Discontinued businesses:	Geothermal Shipbuilding	
New businesses:		Synthetics Real estate

Scale of Operations	1980	1990
Gross revenues ($ millions)	$12,945	$11,812
Employees	48,810	20,930
Shareholders	87,000	65,000

Index